THE VOICES OF ITALY
Italian Language Newspapers and Radio Programs in Rhode Island

Alfred R. Crudale

BORDIGHERA PRESS
NEW YORK, NEW YORK

Robert Viscusi Essay Series
Volume 3

This book series is dedicated to the long essay. It intends to publish those studies that are longer than the traditional journal-length essay and yet shorter than the traditional book-length manuscript.

ISBN 978-1-59954-181-5
Library of Congress Control Number: 2021945112

BORDIGHERA PRESS
John D. Calandra Italian American Institute
25 West 43rd Street, 17th Floor
New York, NY 10038

*I dedicate this book to the memory of my grandparents,
Alfred and Mary Crudale, and Sam and Etta DiSanto,
who instilled in me my pride and love
of our Italian American heritage.*

ACKNOWLEDGEMENTS

I wish to thank the following people whose helped made this book a reality. The staff of the Mary Elizabeth Robinson Research Center at the Rhode Island Historical Society. Professor Peter Covino and Susan Kimmerlein who read my manuscript and gave many helpful suggestions. Antonio Pace's daughter Mary Candito, Claudio Campellone's daughter Marian Campellone Martin, and Rolando Petrella's son John Petrella. Mark Dionne, Archivist at the University of Rhode Island Special Collections. Dr. Ed Ianuccilli. Anthony Julian Tamburri and Nicholas Grosso of Bordighera Press for their guidance and advice.

I especially wish to thank my wife Barbara for her encouragement, love, and patience.

TABLE OF CONTENTS

Introduction

The Voices of Italy

As a young boy, I remember my grandparents often talking about Antonio Pace and his radio program. They would often tell me how happy they were when they first heard Pace speaking Italian on the radio, and how they looked forward to hearing his program each week. They, like many Italians in Rhode Island, were especially fond of Pace's recorded greetings from their families and *paesani* whom they had left in Italy. I also fondly remember listening to Claudio Campellone's *Festa Italiana* and Rolando Petrella's *Voce d'Italia* in my parents' and grandparents' homes, and we always had a copy of *The Italian Echo* newspaper to keep abreast of what was happening in our community. After graduating from Rhode Island College, I began teaching Italian at a local high school and I would often use audio tapes of radio programs, as well as *The Italian Echo* to supplement and augment my lessons.

The state census of 1936 shows almost 10,000 Italians in Rhode Island, and by this time the Italian American community was excited about a new radio program on WPRO hosted by Antonio Pace. Pace's program, *The Italo-American Radio Review*, broadcast in Italian, quickly became very popular among the Italo-Americans in the state and he, along with Claudio Campellone and Rolando Petrella, became one of the pioneers of Italian language radio programming in Southern New England. Their legacy gave rise to the programs hosted by MariaGina Aiello and others whose mission is to promote the Italian culture in our state while keeping the Italo-American community connected to and informed about its roots.

This book grew out of a conference paper which I presented in 2017 at the John D. Calandra Italian American Institute in New York City. Its purpose is to share the history of the Italian language newspapers and radio programs so that the reader may become acquainted with and appreciate the deep pride of Italian culture and the strong sense of Italian heritage which exists among the Italo-American community of Rhode Island. In the first section of *The Voices of Italy* I give a detailed history of *L'Eco del Rhode Island* newspaper, which later became the *Rhode Island Echo*, beginning with the very first edition of the paper in 1897. I examine the Italian immigration, as well as census information regarding the Italian American population in Rhode Island. You will read about changes in ownership and editors of the paper, as well as details on the styles of the paper, specific features, and economic ups and downs. The reader will learn about the current owner and his move to a digital format. You will also read, however, an individual history of six other Italian language newspapers: *La Libertà, L'Alba, The Italian Review, The Rhode Island Italo-American, Italia USA,* and *The Federal Hill Gazette* which also served the Italian American community of Rhode Island.

The Voices of Italy, in its second section, focuses on the Italian language radio programs broadcast in Rhode Island. You will meet the three pioneers of Italian radio programming in the state. Antonio Pace was the initial pioneer of Italian language radio in Rhode Island, as he was the first to produce and announce a radio program in the Italian language for Rhode Island's Italian diaspora. Claudio Campellone, educator, entrepreneur, and radio personality, became one of the essential members of Rhode Island's Italo-American community and his radio program, *La Festa Italiana,* was a favorite among his fellow immigrants. Rolando Petrella produced and announced one of the most popular and longest running Italian radio programs in Rhode Island.

After reading about the story of his life prior to his emigration, as well as his immigration to the United States, you will learn about Petrella's introduction to radio announcing, and how he developed his extremely successful radio program *La Voce d'Italia*

Two young innovative radio announcers changed the format of the traditional Italian radio show in order to appeal to a wider audience. Their target was second, third, and even fourth generation Italian Americans, as well as Italophiles who had limited or no knowledge of the Italian language. MariaGina Aiello is an accomplished woman from Calabria, and the only female to host an Italian radio program in Rhode Island. The reader learns how Aiello transitioned Petrella's *La Voce d'Italia* to a bilingual program to attract new listeners. Johnny Nardo, a third generation Italo-American Rhode Island native, hosts a radio show broadcast mostly in English, which features Italian American entertainers such as Dean Martin, Frank Sinara, and Connie Francis.

In the Epilogue, I introduce readers to lesser-known announcers whose programs aired on smaller stations and did not enjoy the many years of programming as did the aforementioned announcers. I conclude with a brief discussion of the importance of language as the basis of a given culture and I challenge my readers to contemplate how Italian Americans will preserve and promote their culture in the absence of the Italian language.

As you read *The Voices of Italy* you will find some citations from the newspapers written in the original text, which are translated in the footnotes. My decision to preserve the original text was to add authenticity as well as historical perspective to the narrative. *The Voices of Italy* is a fascinating journey through the history of Italian language newspapers and radio programs in Rhode Island. I am excited for you to accompany me on this odyssey as we probe the years of Italian heritage in Rhode Island through her newspapers and radio programs.

Buon viaggio!

PART ONE

THE WRITTEN WORD

Chapter One

THE ECHO

> *After a careful study of the Italian Colony of*
> *Providence, its customs and traits, together with*
> *the interest that it takes and ought to take in public*
> *affairs, I have come to the conclusion that an*
> *Italian newspaper published with the sole*
> *intention of furthering the interest of the Colony*
> *cannot be anything but a success.*[1]
>
> Federico Curzio

In his salutatory of the first issue of the weekly newspaper *L'Eco del Rhode Island*, editor Federico Curzio declares that the "Italian Colony of Providence" had increased to the point where it warranted a media source that focused on and addressed the customs, traits, and interests of the Italian diaspora of Rhode Island. The founders of *L'Eco del Rhode Island* came together to begin to address the journalistic and literary needs of this growing community.[2] In his study on the immigrant press, Robert E. Park argues, "In addition to every other reason for the existence of a foreign-language press is its value to the immigrant, in satisfying his mere human desire for expression in his mother tongue."[3] In the late nineteenth century the Italian diaspora of Rhode Island, having become a substantial immigrant community within the state, yearned for a medium which would reflect their culture, written in their *madre lingua*. In later years this penchant for the Italian language

---

[1] *L'Eco del Rhode Island*, Anno I, no. 1, 1897

[2] The first Rhode Island weekly newspaper written in Italian was entitled *L'Aurora*. It survived only "the winter months of 1895-1896," and thus was a very short-lived endeavor. It was founded by Michele Pesaturo of Providence and was printed by Federico Curzio. No physical copies of this paper are known to exist. See *Italo-Americans of Rhode Island*, Ubaldo U. M. Pesaturo, Visitor Printing Co.: Providence, RI, 1940, 181.

[3] Robert Park, *The Immigrant Press and Its Control*, Harper & Brothers Publishers: New York, 1922, 11.

would manifest itself in radio programs in addition to the Italian language newspapers. Interestingly, the Italian-Americans of Rhode Island in the twenty-first century continue to desire media which preserve and promote the Italian language and culture.

The 1865 and 1875 Rhode Island state censuses do not list Italians as a separate heading under foreign born residents of the state. As there were so few Italian-born residents in Rhode Island (26 total)[4] they are listed under the category "Other Countries." The 1885 state census, however, reports a total of 760 Italian born residents,[5] and categorizes them under the heading "Italy" in the data pertaining to foreign born residents of Rhode Island. The population of Italians in Rhode Island steadily increased, so by 1895 the total number of Italians living in Rhode Island had risen to 5,717.[6] The first decades of the early twentieth century see the greatest influx of immigrants from southern and eastern Europe, and the population of Italians in Rhode Island grew exponentially. In 1911 the Fabre Lines, a French steamship line, operated out of the port of Providence, which resulted in Providence becoming one of the nation's premier immigrant landing facilities.[7] By the 1925 state census, Italians had become the largest ethnic group in Rhode Island with a population recorded at 34,671. The census reports, "During the past decade the Italians have passed the French Canadians as residents of the state by 8,663, the former having gained 7,172, and the latter having lost 2,098."[8] As is evident

---

[4] The Report upon the *Census of Rhode Island 1875* reports 19 males and 7 females. Providence: Providence Press Co., 1877.

[5] See *Rhode Island State Census 1885*, Providence: E.L. Freeman & Sons State Printers, 1887.

[6] See *Census of Rhode Island 1895*, Providence: E.L. Freeman & Sons State Printers, 1898.

[7] Carmela Santoro, *The Italians in Rhode Island: The Age of Exploration to the Present, 1524-1989*, Providence: The Rhode Island Heritage Commission, 1990. / Joseph Muratore, *Italian-Americans in Rhode Island*, New Hampshire: Arcadia Publishing, 1997.

[8] The 1925 Rhode Island State Census, unpublished.

through the census data the Italian diaspora of Rhode Island had become an ever increasing populace in the state, and the Italian newspapers were a fundamental element in the preservation of the Italian culture, as well as the education of the Italian immigrants. "Immigrants who spoke a little broken English or hardly understood a single word of that language relied on ethnic newspapers as their main or even only source of information,"[9] writes Luconi. Park, meanwhile, concludes the foreign-language press played an important role in constructing identities and orienting new immigrants to life in the United States.[10]

The first issue of *L'Eco del Rhode Island* was distributed on Saturday, October 2, 1897. The paper was a weekly publication, distributed every Saturday, free of charge except for postage. In its first year *L'Eco* was distributed in Providence and Newport, as well as, in Boston, Lowell, and Fall River, Massachusetts, in Manhattan, and Brooklyn, New York, and in Pittsburgh, Pennsylvania. Printed in Italian, *L'Eco* provided local news and information about the Italian community of Rhode Island. In his salutatory in the first issue of *L'Eco del Rhode Island* Curzio established four principles upon which the paper is founded, that underscores the maintenance of the Italian language and culture, as well as the goal to assist and educate non-English speaking members of the Italian community. The passage read:

> The present newspaper will be called L'ECO DEL RHODE ISLAND. The main interest of the founders of this paper will be:

---

[9] Stefano Luconi, "The Italian-Language Press, Italian American Voters, and Political Intermediation in Pennsylvania in the Interwar Years." *The International Migration Review*, Vol 33, No. 4 (Winter, 1999), p. 1033.
[10] Robert Park, *The Immigrant Press and Its Control*, New York: Harper & Brothers Publishers (1922).

1st. -- To pacify and mediate all the heated controversies now existing in the colony.

2d. -- To instruct those that lack knowledge of the English
language, in the current affairs of City and State.

3rd. -- To guard the colony from infamous and false
attacks heretofore launched by certain brainless and
know-nothing men.

4th. -- To make public all interesting happenings of the
day.[11]

Beside Curzio's initial goals, the front page of the first
issue of *L'Eco* also reported the wedding of Luisa Zambarano to Pietro Massa, who were married, "Domenica
scorsa, nella Chiesa Italiana, dal Rev. Padre Novati."[12] The
article lists the names of the bride's parents, as well as those
of many of the guests who attended. A description of the
ceremony and reception concludes the article:

> Molte carrozze accompagnarono gli sposi alla Chiesa. La
> sera non mancò la Musica [sic], con gli usuali quattro
> salti."[13]

Following the article about the wedding, is a notice of the
baptism of "una bella e vezzosa bambina"[14] who goes un-
named. The names of the godparents, Il Sig. Frank Storti
and his wife, la signora Maddalena Storti are, however,
found in the announcement. The next notice tells of a
small festival held on September 27 in honor of St. Cosmo
given by Il Sig. Cosmo Bucci. The editors of the paper
conclude the article with wishes of health and prosperity to

---

[11] *L'Eco del Rhode Island,* Anno I, no. 1, 1897.

[12] "Last Sunday, in the Italian Church, by the Reverend Father Novati." *L'Eco del
Rhode Island,* Anno I, no. 1. All translations of quotes from the Italian language
newspapers in this book are done by the author unless otherwise noted.

[13] "Many carriages accompanied the bride and groom to the Church. The evening was
not without music, and the usual dancing." *L'Eco del Rhode Island,* Anno I, no. 1.

[14] "a beautiful and charming baby girl" *L'Eco del Rhode Island,* Anno I, no. 1.

Mr. Bucci: "L'Eco, augura al Sig. Cosmo Bucci salute e dollari."[15] Finally, prominently displayed in the top right corner of the front page is a large advertisement for a liquor store located on Spruce Street in Providence. The ad provides the reader with the address, telephone number and cable number of the Caproni Bros. & Co., which it describes as "Wholesale Liquor Dealers and Bottlers."[16]

Certain alcoholic beverages including wine and specific liqueurs, such as Annisette, Galliano, and Campari were essential to the new immigrants. Wine was drunk at lunch and dinner, and the liqueurs were served to relatives and friends who may come by for a visit. The placement of this ad in a prominent space on the front page underscores the importance of the availability of these items.

After the first month of publication, the editors of *L'Eco del Rhode Island,* began to make changes. While the newspaper remained a weekly publication, it was no longer free to its readers. One could buy *L'Eco* for one cent per copy, or a subscription was offered to readers at twenty-five cents per year. In 1900 *L'Eco* consisted of four pages; the first two providing news and information, and the final two consisted of advertisements. As the popularity and the demand of *L'Eco* increased, so did the price. By August of 1913 the paper had increased to eight pages, and a yearly subscription cost one dollar. The paper continued to be dominated by advertising. These ads were now placed throughout the paper, with the most prominent appearing on the front and back pages. Ads for Dottor O.A. Carella (a surgeon), Farmacia del "Leone," Columbus Exchange Bank, Pasquale Romano (a lawyer), and La

---

[15] "L'Eco, wishes Mr. Bucci health and dollars." *L'Eco del Rhode Island,* Anno I, no. 1. The *onomastico,* or name day is an important Italian tradition in which a child is named after a patron saint. As the child and the saint share a name, a celebration is held on the saint's feast day, and the child usually receives small gifts, such as fruit, a favorite meal, or a small of amount of money (usually coins.) While the practice still exists, it is not as popular today as it was in the past.

[16] *L'Eco del Rhode Island,* Anno I, no. 1.

Caproni Bottling Co., were all displayed on the front page. The back page contained ads for Providence businesses, The Consumer's Brewing Co., Hotel Venezia, and Tripoli Market, as well as The Tosi Music Co. of Boston.

January 1930 ushered in major changes for Rhode Island's foremost Italian newspaper, which included new owners and a new editorial staff. In the first issue dated *3 gennaio 1930*, the paper lists Alexander Bevilacqua as the Managing Editor, and Professor V.E. Cinquegrana as editor. A native of Massachusetts, Bevilacqua moved to Rhode Island after graduating from the School of Journalism at Boston University. Bevelacqua was a well-respected journalist known for "his uncompromising stand against racial bigotry, and through his untiring literary efforts contributed greatly to lifting the prestige of persons of Italian extraction in Rhode Island."[17] In his later years Bevilacqua was inducted into the prestigious Italo-American Society of New York for his "efforts in behalf of things Italian."[18] *The Providence Journal* reported that Bevilacqua, whose name later became Anglicized to Drinkwater, was "known for a sharp pen and a delight for controversy." [19] For a brief period Bevilacqua owned and operated an Italo-American weekly newspaper (which is discussed in Chapter Two), but in 1930, he and his father purchased *L'Eco del Rhode Island*, and immediately began to make changes beginning with the title of the newspaper. The first issue of January 3, 1930 featured a new look as the header had been completely revamped. The new moniker read, in large bold font, *The Italian Echo*, and beneath the title appeared an eagle, wings spread, and holding in its talons two shields; in its right talon, the shield of the USA, and in its left, the medieval shield of the Crusaders. The title

---

[17] *The Italian Echo*, April 16, 1954.
[18] Ibid.
[19] *Providence Journal Obituary*, April 14, 1954.

L'Eco del Rhode Island (in much smaller italicized font) appears above the large font English title. This is a significant change which seems to signal the weekly's evolution into a more assimilated "Italian-American" identity. In his initial editorial, written on the front page, entitled, "Meet the Italian Echo," Bevilacqua writes, "This first issue is but an indication of what the editors have in mind. Many features are to be introduced from time to time, both in Italian and English, embracing every aspect of Italian-American life."[20] In addition to Bevilacqua's editorial/introduction to the new *Echo*, the first page features three articles. The first, written in English, reports on an Italian art exhibition in England. The other two are written in Italian. The more substantial of the two , which would be considered the headline of the newspaper, and which occupies the majority of the front page, is entitled "Il tramonto della Lega Fascista."[21] A scathing rebuke of non-Italians who sought to dissolve the Fascist League of North America, written by Professor Vincenzo E. Cinquegrana, of Brown University, the article laments the demise of the League with harsh words and strong criticism, especially of American journalists and politicians. Cinquegrana's harshest criticism is directed toward Marcus Duffield, a writer for *Harper's Magazine*, whose sensationalistic article entitled "Mussolini's American Empire" is credited with the dissolution of the League. "Dopo le chiassosse fanfaronate dell'illustre ignoto Duffield, incorniciate in quello scomposto mosaico di faterell degni di un cervellino di treccola ciarliera e malignetta,"[22] begins Cinquegrana's article. Following his caustic words for the American journalist, the

---

[20] *The Italian Echo*, Anno XXXVII, No.1. 3 gennaio 1930.
[21] "The Sunset of the Fascist League." *The Italian Echo*, Anno XXXVII, No.1. 3 gennaio 1930. Front page.
[22] "After the noisy boastings of the illustrious unknown Duffield, framed in that haphazard mosaic of irrelevant facts worthy of a tiny brain of a chatty, evil, spiteful noisemaker" Ibid (Translation by author).

professor's tone softens as he praises the Italian ambassador's defense of the League. Finally he returns to his searing critical style blaming the downfall of the organization on "congiure e persecuzioni," (plots and persecutions) as he writes, "Educatori, professionisti intemerati, italiani che per un ventennio, ininterrottamente, con la parola, con la penna, con l'insegnamento han combattuto le più nobili battaglie pel santo nome della Patria – si son visti sopraffatti, insultati, discreditati (almeno ne avevano le intenzioni!) da un arlecchino impomatato ed imbellettato."[23] The final front page article of this issue is a small piece reporting on a protest which took place at Faneuil Hall in Boston.

Along with the changes on the front page, the new *Italian Echo* added several new features such as "Notizie dalle città d'Italia," which reported news from cities throughout Italy. The major change, however, was the "English Feature Section," which occupied two pages and contained a sports section, a theater section, a society column, and a personal section. This combination of Italian and English gave the paper a much broader appeal within the Italian-American community, and underscored the changing paradigm of the Italian diaspora of Rhode Island.

In the late 1920s and into the 1930s the circulation of Italian language newspapers was at an all-time high. *Il Progresso Italo-Americano*, printed in New York by Generoso Pope, boasted the largest circulation in the country with a daily average of approximately 125,000 copies. *Il Corriere d'America*, also owned by Pope, was the second largest in the United States, distributing approximately

---

[23] Educators, consummate professionals, Italians who for twenty years, uninterruptedly, through word, the pen, and teaching have fought the most noble battles for the holy name of the Fatherland – have been seen as defeated, insulted, discredited (at least they had the intentions!) by a slick and prettified Harlequin." Ibid. (Translation by author).

50,000 copies per issue.[24] These were large newspapers which were distributed throughout the northeast, and differed greatly from the small weeklies or bi-weeklies which were the staples of a specific state or region. These widely distributed dailies, however, were examples of the important role which the foreign language press was playing in the post-World War I decades. Much to the chagrin of the mainstream American press, the foreign language newspapers had grown into a staple for foreign born citizens and their descendants. While Park observed that the average American harbored an "instinctive distrust of anything foreign and unintelligible," he also argued that the foreign language press had a great potential to be developed into "an instrument of Americanization."[25] In fact, ethnic newspapers throughout the United States had greatly augmented assimilation of their foreign-born readership.

In a much more recent study published in 2016, Hickerson and Gustafson argue that the immigrant press serves two fundamental functions "The first was to provide civic and cultural explanation" to first generation immigrants. "The second was to promote assimilation and/or citizenship."[26] Leah Moses, owner of the newspaper *Russkaya Obshina i Biznes*, whom they interviewed for their study, confirms that her newspaper for example "builds a bridge between the United States and the Russian-speaking community. People look to her newspaper to understand the culture around them and explain nuances that would be missed if their main source of news were Russian newspapers or TV."[27]

---

[24] Stefano Luconi, "The Italian-Language Press, Italian American Voters, and Political Intermediation in Pennsylvania in the Interwar Years." *The International Migration Review*, Vol 33, No. 4 (Winter, 1999), p. 1050.

[25] *The Immigrant Press and Its Control*, Robert Park, Harper & Brothers Publishers: New York, 1922, p.448.

[26] "Revisiting the Immigrant Press. Andrea Hickerson, Kristin L. Gustafson. *Journalism* 2016, Vol.17 (8), p. 952.

[27] Ibid.

In the April 17, 1931 issue of *The Italian Echo*, Alexander Bevilacqua expounds on this theme in an editorial commentary entitled "The Foreign Language Press." His initial paragraph acknowledges the hostilities of mainstream America toward the ethnic press in which he writes, "So we find the good ladies of the D.A. R. [sic] (Daughter of the American Revolution) and some Congressmen seeing 'red,' each time they come across a newspaper printed in a foreign language."[28] He argues, however, in the successive paragraphs that the foreign language newspapers had been instrumental in "Americanizing" their readers long before certain professional agencies began the process. Emphasizing the strong pride in their heritage and having developed into "an institution of great influence and power," Bevilacqua concludes his editorial with the prophecy that the "foreign language press has years of usefulness ahead of it and through the medium of a national association its program can be one of great constructive worth."[29]

A mere four months later *The Italian Echo* acquired a new editor who would champion the Italian language not only in print, but in the not-so-distant future, on the radio as well. The August 21, 1931 issue of *The Italian Echo* named Antonio Pace as the editor. Pace, a pillar of the Italo-American community of Rhode Island (and the subject of Chapter Three) initiates his tenure with an editorial column on the front page of the paper in which he promotes the study of the Italian language, not only among young people, but across all segments of the diaspora. In his opening paragraph he outlines the benefits of the study of Italian. "Lo studio della lingua italiana," writes Pace, "s'impone ai giovani studenti della nostra razza, non solo per i benefici diretti che da essa derivano, ma anche per un dovere sociale verso la famiglia e perché mantiene

---

[28] The Italian Echo, Anno XXXVIII, venerdì, 17 aprile 1931.
[29] Ibid.

saldi i vincoli di razza, la cui compatezza [sic] è elemento essenziale di civiltà e progresso per la nostra patria di adozione."[30] In his editorial Pace argues that the American government seeks young people who speak and write Italian, following up his statement with a list of occupations from the State Department to translators and interpreters. The study of the Italian language, he passionately reminds his readers in his closing paragraph, is an obligation which must be taken seriously. Pace's concern for the promotion of the Italian language was quite apropos for change was already in the air. Following two acts of Congress in the early 1920s, the Emergency Quota Act of 1921, and the National Origins Quota Act of 1924, immigration from Italy drastically declined. "These discriminatory measures," writes Carmela Santoro, "were designed to restrict the number of newer immigrants (particularly Italians, Jews, and Slavs) to the United States. With the help of a global economic depression and the Second World War, these laws accomplished the intent of their xenophobic sponsors."[31] The 1924 law set the annual immigration quota from Italy at 6,000[32] which had devastating results for the Italian diaspora both nationally and in Rhode Island.

As the number of first-generation Italians decreased, more and more English crept into the everyday lives of the Italo-American community. While the majority of the *Italian Echo* continued to be printed in Italian, more sections and features were slowly transitioning to English, as

---

[30] "The study of the Italian language is imposed on the youth of our race, not only for the direct benefits which they obtain, but also for a social obligation toward the family and because it maintains stable bonds to our race, whose solidarity is an essential element of civilization and progress for our country of adoption." *The Italian Echo*, Friday, August 21, 1931. Front page.
[31] *The Italians in Rhode Island: The Age of Exploration to the Present 1524-1989*. Carmela E. Santoro. Providence: The Rhode Island Heritage Commision, 1990.
[32] *La Storia: Five Centuries of the Italian American Experience.* Jerre Mangione, Ben Morreale. New York: Harper Collins Publishers, Inc., 1992, p. 316.

was the case with many of the immigrant newspapers throughout the country. Such a transition is a natural result of assimilation. Second and third generation, immersed in the language and culture of their new country, are less dependent on the *madre lingua* spoken by their first-generation relatives. Ties to the *patria* (fatherland) become increasingly less important as the younger generation is influenced daily by the American media culture. As the older generation passes on, more and more ethnic newspapers are printed in English.[33] Thus, foreign language newspapers undergo significant changes to attract and maintain their readership, as they target the first, second, third, and in fact all generations of their particular diaspora. The *Italian Echo* was no exception. By January of 1935, in only 38 years, *The Italian Echo* was now a four-page weekly in which the first two pages were written in Italian and the final two written in English. On March 29, however, the headlines of *The Echo* announce a "Nuovo Proprietario dell'Eco," (New Owner of the *Eco)* who is introduced to his readers in a lengthy editorial written in Italian on the front page. Described as "giovane, intelligentissimo e pieno di belle iniziative,"[34] Luigi Picerno, owner and operator of Broadway Press, is named as the new owner of *The Italian Echo*. Explaining the intentions of the new owner, the editorial (most likely written by Antonio Pace) states that Picerno wants to make the paper "una pubblicazione che veramente risponde ai fini e agli interessi della nostra co-munità."[35] These words are reinforced by the content and subsequent editorials. The newspaper begins to print their editorials in both Italian (on the front page) and English inside the paper. Now an eight-page weekly, *The Italian*

---

[33] "The Future of Ethnic Newspapers in the United States and Canada." Faye Leibowitz. *Serials Review.* June 2012, Vol. 38 Issue 2, p. 105.

[34] "young, extremely intelligent, and full of wonderful initiatives"

[35] "a publication which truly responds to the needs and interests of our commu-nity."

Echo features more news of the community and the world in English, as well as a sports section and one or two comic strips. "The Battling Browns" is a spoof on the trials and tensions of a married couple. It was part of a comic strip, drawn and written by Rube Goldberg, entitled "Cartoon Follies." The paper also included a one panel strip entitled "Just Humans" written by Gene Carr, which served as a satirical commentary on the ills of society. Later two episodic series strips were added. "Detective Riley" is attributed to Richard Lee, while "Dash Dixon," a sci fi series was written and drawn by Dean Carr.

Under the direction of Picerno *The Italian Echo* continued to evolve, but there also seemed to be a growing tension between the Italian diaspora, presumably represented by *The Italian Echo*, and those outside the Italian-American community. On September 29, 1935, the paper ran an editorial entitled "Drowning Discordant Voices," in which they report a meeting of various statewide Italian organizations which took place at the headquarters of the Sons of Italy on Tuesday, September 24, 1935. Reportedly, at this meeting the "representatives of the various Italian organizations throughout the State"[36] rallied in support of Benito Mussolini regarding the "Italo-Ethiopian question"[37] The editorial affirms that "[If] anyone doubted the status of local Italians in the matter, they would have been quickly educated as to their true feelings during the tumultuous and patriotic manifestation of loyalty and fervor."[38] After a list of atrocities and savage practices supposedly perpetrated by the Ethiopian regime, the editors urge that "the other presumably civilized nations should cooperate with Mussolini in bringing peace and comfort to that strife-torn and unenlightened country."[39] During the mid 1930s and into

---

[36] *The Italian Echo*, Friday, September 27, 1935, Editorial.
[37] Ibid.
[38] Ibid.
[39] Ibid.

1940, the national Italian-American press promoted Mussolini, and encouraged their readers to support Il Duce, who (they believed) was responsible for restoring glory to Italy and the modern Roman empire, filling the Italian immigrants in America with great pride.

Italian-American newspapers throughout the United States, taking their lead from Generoso Pope's *Il Progresso* of New York, garnered support and enthusiasm for the Fascists.[40] These very newspapers received news and information about Italy from the Stefani press agency, which was based in Rome, and controlled by the Fascist regime.[41] Luconi states that "the editors and publishers of Italian-American newspapers themselves offered to extol fascism in their publications in exchange for the purchase of ads by ENIT (the Italian tourist information office) and other Italian state-controlled agencies and companies."[42] As early as December of 1935 *The Italian Echo* printed an editorial directed specifically at Rhode Island Governor Theodore Francis Green, entitled "Anti-fascist means anti-Italian, Governor Green."[43]

By 1941, however, the pro-Fascist Italian language newspapers began to abandon Mussolini in favor of a much more patriotic, pro-America rhetoric. After having declared war on the United States, Mussolini's support quickly dissipated, and disappeared altogether upon his decision to go to war alongside Adolf Hitler.[44]

June 14, 1940, signals another change to RI's premiere Italian language newspaper, the most significant being a

[40] *La Storia: Five Centuries of the Italian American Experience.* Jerre Mangione, Ben Morreale. New York: Harper Collins Publishers, Inc., 1992, p. 319.
[41] Stefano Luconi. "The Italian-Language Press, Italian American Voters, and Political Intermediation in Pennsylvania in the Interwar Years." *The International Migration Review*, Vol. 33, No. 4 (Winter, 1999), pp. 1039-1039.
[42] Ibid., p. 1039.
[43] The Italian Echo, Friday, December 20, 1935.
[44] *La Storia: Five Centuries of the Italian American Experience.* Jerre Mangione, Ben Morreale. New York: Harper Collins Publishers, Inc., 1992, p. 322.

new name. Now *The Rhode Island Echo* (a nod to its original title), the front page is bilingual as articles are written in both English and Italian, with the headlines in Italian. The cost of the paper is five cents per copy, and lists Vincent Sorrentino as "President and Treasurer," and Claudio L. Campellone, publisher. The paper consists of eight pages, with several new components of information "La Cronica del New England" (p.2), a feature which provides news and information about cities throughout New England. On page four readers find "Il Calendario" filled with dates and times of important events in and around Rhode Island. "The Passing Show: Presenting the World in Pictures" (p. 5) is a series of captioned photographs of countries throughout the world. On page six readers find two novels written in Italian as a series of installments which continue weekly. One is entitled *Il Conte Grimani* (*Count Grimaldi*), authored by Giorgio Carredi, while Francesco Mastriani writes the second novel, *La Cieca di Sorrento* (*The Blind Woman of Sorrento*). The final two pages of the *Rhode Island Echo*, written in English, contain a sports section called "Sportscope," and a section dedicated to women's fashion entitled "Women's Bazaar." With its new name, section heading, and its expanded content *The Rhode Island Echo* establishes itself as one of Rhode Island's leading weekly newspapers, as well as an essential source of news, information, and entertainment for the Italo-American community of the state.

A mere nine months later, however, the paper experiences yet another name change. This time returning to its roots with the new title *L'Eco d'America* which appears on the front page of the February 14, 1941 edition. *L'Eco d'America* was an Italian language weekly which began publication in 1894. Very little is known about the paper as no editions from the 1890s seem to exist. Vincent Lapomarda dedicates one sentence to *L'Eco d'America* in *The Italian American Experience: An Encyclopedia*, writing,

"*L'Eco d'America* (1894) ... a weekly that appears to be the precursor to *L'Eco del Rhode Island* (1897)."[45] In his welcome statement in the first edition of his paper, Federico Curzio mentions the existence of an Italian weekly newspaper prior to *L'Eco del Rhode Island*, but he does not offer the title or provide any information regarding the editors. He does, however, inform his readers that the previous paper failed.[46] By April of 1941 *L'Eco d'America* merges with a smaller, less popular weekly entitled *The Italian American Tribune*, which was owned by Antonio Pace and printed in Providence, but only for an extremely brief period, until the merger with *L'Eco d'America*. Following the merger both titles appear on the front page. *L'Eco d'America* in big bold font, with *The Italian American Tribune* in small bold font beneath it. The May 23, 1941 edition, however, no longer uses *The Italian American Tribune* title, and thus marks the demise of that extremely short lived Italo-American weekly newspaper. *L'Eco d'America* meanwhile continues to circulate as such until 1947 at which time, under editor Francis Del Deo and publisher Louis Picerno, it once again becomes *The Italian Echo*. Picerno continues to publish the paper under this title until 1969, which seems to signal the end of the newspaper. While the paper begins the year on January 3, 1969 with Volume 73, on December 19, 1969 Picerno publishes his final issue. As the ink dries in the presses, the Italian American community of Rhode Island will wait for three months before they once again enjoy a weekly newspaper that serves their specific community.

---

[45] The Italian American Experience: An Encyclopedia. Salvatore J. LaGumina, editor. New York: Garland Publishers, 2000.

[46] "It is not a new conception, it has been tried before, and has failed: but the ideas of the gentleman who undertakes to publish L'ECO DEL RHODE ISLAND, differs entirely from those of the gentlemen who were interested in previous enterprises of this sort." *L'Eco del Rhode Island*, Anno I, no. 1.

Finally on March 26, 1970, under the direction of Antonio Pace, and his son, Harold Pace as editor, *The Echo: The Italo-American Voice of Rhode Island* makes its long-anticipated return. While the title has changed, the first issue boasts, in the left corner of the front page, Volume 74, indicating to its loyal readers that this paper continues the proud lineage of *L'Eco del Rhode Island*. In a front page editorial, the Paces assure readers that *The Echo* will "serve as a link, a much needed binding force among Italo-Americans in this state. It will be a newspaper not only for its readers, but, to a great extent, by its readers."[47] The now famous radio personality, Antonio Pace and his son Harold produced an extremely professional and increasingly sophisticated publication. For a yearly subscription of $4.00 readers received an eight page weekly featuring news from Rhode Island, the United States, and Italy; information regarding the surrounding communities; and an engagement and wedding section. As the year progressed the editor added new features, and in July of 1970 a special feature entitled "Publisher's Memoirs" was introduced. Each week, as the title suggests, Antonio Pace would recount his life story to his readers, the highlights of which are discussed in the third chapter of this book.

In January of 1971 the Paces introduced a column entitled "The Federal Hill Story." This feature quickly became very popular with the readers of *The Echo*, as it showcased Rhode Island's "Little Italy." The column was written by Tony Marrocco as he recounted history and local stories about "the old neighborhood." Some of the topics Marrocco covered were local show business, the pushcart peddlers, the drugstores of Federal Hill, the milkman, and the fisherman. Often readers would contribute personal stories and photos, which Marrocco would incorporate into his weekly column.

---

[47] *The Echo*, Vol. 74, No.1. Front Page.

Neither the "Publisher's Memoirs," nor "The Federal Hill Story," however, could help the Paces sustain *The Echo*, and in January of 1972, the paper once again changed hands, this time sold to Emilio Roberti (R.E. Roberti). In the February 3, 1972 issue of *The Echo*, editor Francis Del Deo made a plea to Rhode Island's Italo-American community for financial support of *The Echo*, which was a sixteen page weekly, and cost fifteen cents a copy. Del Deo's pitch seems to have worked, and new life was breathed into *The Echo*. A new header consisted of the phrase The Italo-American Voice of Rhode Island in small print just above the words The Echo in large bold print. To the right of the header four overlapping images of the map of Rhode Island, also graced the newspaper. Roberti's staff began to expand the paper to a 43-page publication featuring, apart from news and information, an Italian language section, an obituary page, a classified section, a sports page, and comics. *The Echo* was at its largest size in the history of the newspaper and rivaled most of the local mainstream weeklies in circulation. For four years *The Echo* continued as one of Rhode Island's leading newspapers, until on April 14, 1977, the publisher issued Volume 80, #13, the final issue of this chapter of *The Echo* history. Once again, the presses went quiet, and Rhode Island's Italian Americans were once more without an ethnic newspaper.

Enter Rhode Island retail magnate Joseph A. Agostinelli. Just as Antonio and Harold Pace had done in 1970, Agostinelli, in 1977, came to the rescue of *The Echo*. In the spring of 1977 Agostinelli, one of the founders of the Rhode Island chapter of United Italian Americans (UNI-TAM), distressed over the demise of *The Echo*, was determined to produce an Italian American newspaper which would not only serve the Italo-American community, but simultaneously pay homage to "the hard work and sacrifices of his grandparents and parents, who were typical of all the immigrants who came to this country in the early

1900s."[48] Agostinelli entered into a bidding war with a local newspaper owner, with the intention of becoming the new owner of *The Echo*. The newspaper man ceased submitting bids when Agostinelli offered $100,000.00 for the paper. Having acquired *The Echo*, Agostinelli opened an office on Atwells Avenue in the Federal Hill section of Providence, from where editor Dean Whitten and his staff expanded the size of the paper and produced one of the most distinguished and professional ethnic newspapers in Rhode Island. In his initial editorial commentary Agostinelli made a direct appeal to his readers in which he stated in part, "I believe that *The Echo* can join with existing Italian American groups in an effort to continue and hopefully, increase the promotion of cultural events. But most importantly, *The Echo* must be used as a vehicle to pass on to our children the rich heritage which is their birthright." Agostinelli entitled his salutatory, "An Italo-American Echo, Once And For All," and it was printed in both English and Italian. During the time Agostinelli owned *The Echo* the paper was comprised of three sections with an average of 72 pages. As Muratore reports, *The Echo* had become one of Rhode Island's leading publications, and one of the largest bilingual newspapers in the United States(8). In an interview, Joseph Agostinelli reveals that due to its popularity and its professionalism, many local politicians sought endorsements by *The Echo* during election years, one of the most famous was the 1980 Rhode Island governor's race between incumbent J. Joseph Garrahy, and Providence mayor, Vincent "Buddy" Cianci. Ultimately Agostinelli decided to give the paper's endorsement to Garrahy, which he remembers as a mistake. Agostinelli states that he should have forgone any endorsement in that race.

---

[48] See Joseph Muratore's column entitled "The Landmarks of Federal Hill" in *The Echo*, November 29, 1979, p. 18.

Under Agostinelli's direction *The Echo*, in addition to the news and information, added engagements and wedding announcements, death notices, society pages, and sports pages, many features which seemed to resonate with its readers. "La Vita Nostra" column was written in Italian and focused on specific aspects of Italian American life. "Kid's Kingdom" with its coloring page, word puzzles, and short stories, targeted children and young readers. News and information regarding Rhode Island entertainment and local talent, including reviews of plays and musicals on stage at the Ocean State Performing Arts Center, Trinity Square Repertory Theater, and the Veterans Memorial Auditorium, was written by Don Fowler and covered in his "That's Entertainment" column. In 1980, in celebration of the new decade, *The Echo* added a "pull out section" entitled "Lifestyle 80" which presented pages on cooking, fashion, home life, nutrition, and home care.

By the summer of 1984 Agostinelli's tenure with *The Echo* was on the wane, as he began to venture into condominium development. One day in a discussion with Rhode Island developer Richard Baccari, Agostinelli learned that Baccari was interested in purchasing *The Echo*, as he believed the paper was an essential element to the Italo-American community of the state. Having concluded negotiations, Agostinelli's final issue was published on January 14, 1984, and Volume 87, No. 4, listed Richard P. Baccari as publisher, and John J. O'Toole as editor. Unlike previous changes in ownership, which had been marked by interruptions of production, the Agostinelli-Baccari transition was a seamless transaction which kept the publication in print.

Richard Baccari was committed to producing the same professional publication which *The Echo* had become, as he stated in his "Letter from the Publisher" in his first issue; "As the publisher of *The Echo*, I am committed to developing this newspaper into one of the finest weekly newspapers in New England."[49] With his stated objective Baccari expanded the newspaper's staff, and began to add features which the staff believed would appeal to a broader audience, while continuing to maintain the Italian and Italian American essence of the paper. Several featured informational columns about Italy and famous Italians, all contributed to the popularity of the newspaper including the Advice column "Ask The Echo," the fashion column "Accents," the entertainment column "Galleria," and the popular "Attenzione" feature. As the 1980s wore on, *The Echo* not only saw changes in editors and other staff positions, but the appearance of the paper also underwent several updates. March 22, 1984 brought with it a modernized header, which simply read *The Echo*, with the word *Echo* appearing in large Italic font. Gone were the previous references to the paper's origins or it being the voice of the Italian American community. Editor Doreen DiMitri included a general interest column entitled "Doreen," in which she opined on a wide variety of topics, such as Gary Trudeau and Doonsbury, Charles Dickens, and fashion. In one of her columns entitled "Embracing Tradition and Moving On," she wrote about the changing role of Italian American women in the 1980s. In an interview Dimitri (presently Doreen Picozzi) reveals that she cherishes many fond memories of her time with *The Echo*. "Richard Baccari is a wonderful man, and we had a great staff. So many dedicated professionals worked very hard to ensure *The Echo* was a publication Italian Americans throughout the state could be proud of" she states.[50]

Besides new features such as "Inside Track," "Buon appetito," and "Homemakers Clinic," the paper added a Section B, called "La Vita Bella" which contained the arts

---

[49] *The Echo*, Vol. 87, No. 4, January 28, 1984, Front page.
[50] This quote is taken from a phone interview between the author and Doreen Dimitri-Picozzi, who presently teaches journalism in the Lincoln Public School District, in Rhode Island.

and entertainment section, the bridal section, and news about the Italian community of Rhode Island. In 1991, Baccari hired popular Rhode Island author and Federal Hill historian Joe Fuoco as editor, and by January 1993, the format of *The Echo* had changed from a traditional broadside format to a compact tabloid format. Fuoco wrote a general interest column entitled "Joe's Place," and Arnoldo Abatecola contributed with a bilingual column with news and information from Italy entitled "Italy's Corner/Angolo d'Italia." The paper continued to be a greatly respected professional publication, which provided local, national, and international news and information. During election years *The Echo* was a great source of information regarding candidates and referenda. Through in-depth interviews with candidates, the paper sought to encourage a well informed electorate among its readership. The writers of *The Echo* provided their readers with compelling and thought-provoking articles One example is the two part article entitled, "Will the Italian Language Survive in Rhode Island?," which appeared in the January 27, 1995 issue. The article examined the interest in the study of Italian in Rhode Island schools. It featured interviews with professors of Italian from the University of Rhode Island, Providence College, and Brown University, and concluded that the interest among students in the state at both the secondary schools and the universities to study the Italian language was not only strong but was likely to endure well into the future.

Unfortunately, the future of *The Echo* did not look as bright. In 1994 the paper started shrinking in size and staff, and by January of 1995 the Baccari era seemed to be coming to an end. *The Echo*, under the direction of Richard Baccari, printed its final issue on March 24, 1995. Unable to find a buyer, Baccari closed down production, and *The Echo* slipped into the annals of Rhode Island history. For seventeen years *The Echo* remained out of print. However, as had happened to this newspaper so many times previously, along came someone who desired to restore this Rhode Island Italo-American icon to it past glory. The name of this latest champion is Robert D'Uva, a local businessman, Chairman of the Board of the DaVinci Center of Providence, and a member of the Italo-American Club of Rhode Island. D'Uva's pride in his Italian heritage lead him not only to revive *The Echo*, but to transform the paper into a 21st- century publication, which includes a website centered on the Italo-American community of Rhode Island. Having previously been co-editor of the *Federal Hill Gazette*, (a newspaper which is discussed in the following chapter) D'Uva brought experience and knowledge of his readership to the *Rhode Island Echo*, a title which pays homage to the original title of the paper, *L'Eco del Rhode Island*. Having already witnessed the economic woes and demise of previous Italian American newspapers, D'Uva provides his paper to the Italian American community of Rhode Island free of charge.

The *Rhode Island Echo*, a monthly publication, is financially sustained through advertisements, which are thoughtfully laid out so as not encroach upon content. Published in the compact tabloid format, the front page of the newspaper, as well as all photographs and advertisements are printed in color, while articles and columns are in black ink. Presently *The Rhode Island Echo* is a 55 page newspaper featuring many interesting and informative columns. The "Food & Drink" section of the paper hosts Jean Restivo's "Cucina di Nonna" column which offers traditional and non-traditional Italian recipes. The section also boasts a wine column by Armando Bisceglia, and restaurant reviews. "Community" is the largest section, and focuses on news and information about the Italian American community of Rhode Island. This section features several popular columns such as "I Remember" by Luo

Marciano, "Rhode Island Profiles" by J. Michael Levesque, and the very popular "La Pagina Italiana" written by Daniela Ciccone and Luo Turchetta. Other sections of *The Rhode Island Echo* include a pet advice page, "Arts & Entertainment," and "Health & Welfare."

Publisher Robert D'Uva admits that overhead is the biggest expense in publishing the paper. He adds, "the key to making this a great paper is multi-tasking,"[51] at which he says he has become an expert. D'Uva's ability to multi-task has restored *The Rhode Island Echo* to its place of prominence, as one of the leading publications of the state. In addition to the monthly distribution of the newspaper, D'Uva and his staff also produce a very professional and user friendly website, *therhodeislandecho.com*, to which readers are able to subscribe free of charge. Presently the website is comprised of seven links. On the homepage appear the latest edition of the newspaper, announcements, a link to subscribe to the website, an archive cleverly called "The Rhode Island Echo Bookcase," and embedded videos germane to the newspaper and the Italo-American community of the state. The other links are an "About" link, a "Monthly Contest" link, the "Latest Issue" link, at which readers are able to read the paper in its entirety, and three other informational links. Web mistress Deana Grenier explains that the website provides the paper to those who either don't come to Providence very often or live out of state. She adds that subscribers to the website (in excess of 6,000) receive a monthly "email blast" which informs them that the most recent edition of *The Rhode Island Echo* is available. The paper also boasts a Facebook page with over 5,000 followers according to Granier. Those readers who like the page enjoy access to videos, announcements of local interest, and selected pages from the *Rhode Island Echo*.

---

[51] Taken from a phone interview between the author and Robert D'Uva.

In this digital era, as printed newspapers struggle to remain relevant and viable, Robert D'Uva,[52] Deana Grenier, and the entire staff of *The Rhode Island Echo* produce a publication, both in print and digitally, which has become a source of great pride to the Italian American community in Rhode Island. *The Rhode Island Echo*, now in its 105th year, owes a great deal of gratitude to Robert D'Uva and his staff for their experience, dedication, and pride in their Italo-American heritage, for it is through them that *The Rhode Island Echo* not only survives, but thrives.

---

[52] Robert D'Uva died unexpectedly on February 18, 2021.

Chapter Two

WEEKLIES, BI-WEEKLIES, AND MONTHLIES

a weekly newspaper of free expression for
people of Italian nativity and extraction.
Alexander Bevilacqua

La Libertà

August 16, 1901 marked the initiation of another Italian language newspaper focused on the Italian-American community of Rhode Island. *La Libertà* was a weekly publication which originally sold for two cents per copy ("*una copia 2 soldi*") or an annual subscription for one dollar. The paper was housed at 300 Atwells Avenue, Providence, RI, and F. Moracci was listed as *direttore*. Above the title, *La Libertà*, which appeared in large Italic font, the subtitle reads "The Only Newspaper in Italian Language in the State of Rhode Island." As we have seen in the first chapter this was an inaccurate claim, as *L'Eco del Rhode Island* was also published in Italian in 1901. Interestingly, this declaration was written in English. Immediately beneath the title, one notes the words "Giornale Settimanale Repubblicano" (Weekly Republican Newspaper). While providing the Rhode Island Italian diaspora with news and information about Italy and Providence, *La Libertà* also featured advertisements for local businesses and services. Consisting of four pages, the front page offered a mix of news and ads, the second page housed a news column entitled "Notizie d'Italia," and a novelette series, written in Italian, entitled "Buona Fortuna — un romanzo italiano" (Good Luck — an Italian novel). Pages three and four were reserved for advertising.

The first two years for *La Libertà* seem to have been quite successful, however, by midyear of 1903 a flurry of changes in ownership and managers had taken place. It is not clear what caused these changes, but beginning with the January 31, 1903 issue C. Mazzinghi Co. is listed as editor, which changes to the A. Pisco Co. beginning with the February 21, 1903 issue. By May 2, 1903 the editor and proprietor is listed as C. Bello, however, by July 11, 1903 V. Talamini buys the paper and moves the operation to 155 Atwells Avenue, Providence, RI. Talamini expanded the paper to eight pages, but maintained the subscription and copy rates ($1.00/year, 2 cents/copy). He replaced the declaration above the title with "The Most Influential Italian Newspaper in the State of Rhode Island," and beneath the title he added *"Unione, Benevolenza, e Concordia"* (Union, Benevolence, and Harmony); beneath these words, in a smaller font he added *"Giornale Settimanale degli Operai"* (Weekly Newspaper of the Workers). The paper continued to be published in Italian, and as the subtitle suggests is geared toward Italian American laborers. Talamini owned and operated the paper from 1903 until its demise in 1909. The final issue of *La Libertà* is issued on Saturday, December 25, 1909.[53]

L'Alba

Marco A. Russo immigrated from San Fele, Italy in 1886. Following a brief period in New York, he moved to Rhode Island, and settled in Newport. After several years as a barber, he established the Russo Advertising and Publishing Company, which began to publish an Italian language newspaper in 1910 under the title *L'Alba (The Dawn)*. The paper began as a Providence based newspaper with its office at 67 Brayton Avenue. The title appeared in

---

[53] While there are no known paper issues of *La Libertà*, the Rhode Island Historical Society Library has microfilm which contain issues July 5, 1902 up to the final issue of December 25, 1909. In his book *Italo-Americans of Rhode Island*, Ubaldo Pesaturo claims that *La Libertà* was in print until 1922, however, I have been unable to substantiate his claim.

large bold decorative font, and immediately beneath it in smaller block letters the words *Giornale Settimanale Indipendente* (Weekly Independent Newspaper). In the right-hand corner, on the same line as the subtitle Marco A. Russo, the proprietor's name appears.

Consisting of eight pages, *L'Alba* offered news from Italy, as well as local news and information. A subscription was one dollar per year, and a single copy cost two cents. A "foreign" subscription could be purchased at the cost of two dollars per year. At the top of page two, among the editorial information, the paper boasted its membership in the American Association of Foreign Language Newspapers. The front page and headlines focused on the latest news from Italy, as well as two large advertisements, the most prominent was the Columbus Exchange Bank of Providence, which occupied the lower right-hand quarter of the page. Page two carried the editorial and subscription information, along with information about Rhode Island and the Italian diaspora of the state. Pages three and four offered news of Providence and the surrounding cities, while the fifth and sixth pages were reserved for advertising, legal advice, and information as to where to obtain specific professional services such as medical, legal, and notary public services. Page seven offered a column entitled, "A Punta di Spillo," (Pinpoint) which was a series of jokes and humorous short stories. Page eight carried a column entitled *Cronaca d'Italia*, which reported more news from Italy, and a novelette series, *Vigilia di Nozze* (The Night before the Wedding), written in Italian.

On June 2, 1915, the subtitle of the paper changed to read "Giornale Semi-weekly Indipendente." The headline read:

EXTRA!
L'ALBA
Cominciando da oggi, uscirà

DUE VOLTE LA
SETTIMANA.[54]

With this issue the newspaper was now distributed twice a
week and sold at one cent per copy. Then on January 1,
1916, the subtitle, now written in English, read "Tri-weekly
Independent Newspaper." Marco Russo's newspaper, still
printed mostly in Italian, with some ads and information in
English, seemed to be enjoying success, however, a tri-weekly
newspaper may have been too ambitious. The November
25, 1916 edition of *L'Alba*, carried the subtitle, in English,
"Weekly Independent Newspaper," and directly beneath, in
an ad type format, an explanation with the title, AVVISO,
that "...l'aumento esorbitante della carta...,"[55] among other
contributing factors the high price of paper had caused the
publisher to return the newspaper to a weekly format.

Beginning with the May 26, 1916 edition, *L'Alba* published, in the center of the front page, an appeal to young
men to join the American Armed Forces, as the United
States was being drawn into the "war to end all wars,"
World War I. The appeal read as follows:

> GIOVANI!
> Oggi è il momento,
>> PER CHI VUOLE BENE
>> ALLA PATRIA, DI DIMOSTRARE
>> L'AMORE
>> CHE SI HA PER ESSA.
> L'AMERICA
>> VUOLE UOMINI NELL'
>> ESERCITO E NELLA
>> MARINA. VOLETE VOI

---

[54] EXTRA! L'ALBA beginning today, will come out TWICE A WEEK.
[55] ...the exorbitant increase in the price of paper...,

ARRUOLARVI?
OGGI E' IL MOMENTO.[56]

This appeal was moved to the second and third pages in subsequent issues.

With the September 20, 1919 edition, *L'Alba* entered a new phase of development. The office and operations were moved from Providence to Newport as the paper began to reflect changes in the Italo-American community. It is important to note that Newport hosts a large Italian American population. Marco A. Russo, one of the original organizers of the Forum Lodge 391 of the Order of the Sons of Italy in Newport, was a leader in the Italo-American community. Publishing his newspaper in Newport, Russo underscored the importance of the Italian diaspora outside of Providence. *L'Alba* continued to be a strong presence and serve the Rhode Island Italian community both on the mainland and in the East Bay.

The November 29, 1919 issue brought further change to *L'Alba*. The font of the title was changed to an Art Deco style, but more importantly, beneath the subtitle a phrase which had not previously graced the paper's moniker appeared. It read: "Consolidate with 'Il Corriere della Sera.'" In an effort to augment his publication, and quite possibly for financial reasons as well, Russo had merged his paper with the well-known Italian paper *Il Corriere della Sera*. It is unclear as to the effect this move had on the readership or the popularity of *L'Alba*, but the two newspapers remained partners until 1936. Interestingly, despite the consolidation with *Il Corriere*, English began to be more prominent in *L'Alba*. The number of articles and advertisements written in English were on the increase, and

---

[56] "YOUNG MEN! Today is the time (moment), FOR WHOEVER LOVES THE COUNTRY, TO SHOW THE LOVE THAT YOU HAVE FOR HER. AMERICA WANTS MEN IN THE ARMY AND IN THE NAVY. DO YOU WANT TO ENLIST? TODAY IS THE TIME (MOMENT)."

while most of the paper continued to be written in Italian, change was on the horizon. An article, written in English, entitled, "The Foreign Language Press and Its Function in America" ran in the January 3, 1920 edition of *L'Alba*. It argued that the foreign language press in the United States was "a stone in the foundation of our industry," responsible for perpetuating the ideals of liberty, independence, and "that hatred of hypocritical pretense." The concluding sentences of the article suggested that without the foreign language press the languages of the immigrants would cease to exist in the U.S. "And what is the main influence that keeps that language alive in our country, and transmits it from generation? It is the foreign press."[57]

By December of 1921 the front page of the paper was bilingual, with the left half of the page written in Italian, and the right half in English. By the new year 1922 the front page was printed entirely in English. Pages two, three, and four were bilingual, and the paper had added a novelette by the famous Russian author, Leo Tolstoi, entitled *Un Povero Diavolo (A Poor Devil)*, which was offered in Italian. The January 1930 issue suggests *L'Alba* was written exclusively in English, and featured a crossword puzzle, comics, and a classified section. Russo also began to encourage Italian immigrants to become citizens of the United States. In each issue on page two (written in Italian) he offered arguments in favor of American citizenship, and a lengthy list of questions and answers to the Citizenship Test, "DOMANDE E RISPOSTE Per divenire Cittadini Americani."[58]

---

[57] *L'Alba*, January 3, 1920. Page 3.

[58] Some examples of Russo's arguments are 1) Solamente essendo cittadino potete esercitare la vostra influenza sulle leggi del paese. (Only by being a citizen can you exercise your influence on the laws of the country.) 2) Essendo cittadino sarete piú [sic] rispettato. (Being a citizen, you will be more respected.) 3) Essendo cittadino non avrete seccature né voi né la vostra famiglia nel caso che vi rechiate in Italia quando ritornerete negli Stati Uniti. (Being a citizen neither you nor your family will have any problems if you go to Italy when you return to

Beginning in June of 1936, a dispute arises between Russo and a Newport alderman, John Mahan, regarding a license for which Russo had applied, and was refused. Russo had applied for a license to establish and operate a "victualing house" on the corners of Spring and Touro Streets; however, it was denied on the grounds that it was too close to a place of worship.[59] Russo airs his grievance on the front page of the July 11, 1936 issue of *L'Alba* with a poorly written headline; "Because We have not been able to find THE NAME OF THE DOCTORS who OPPOSES Marco A. Russo LICENCE CANN0T PRINT THIS Week the news."[60] The dispute seems to signal trouble for Russo and his newspaper. In each edition of *L'Alba*, Russo uses the front page to attack and harras Alderman Mahan, as well as the mayor, Henry S. Wheeler. As the year trudges on, so do Russo's attacks, as his headlines become repetitive and stale. In the November 21, 1936 issue the lengthy and verbose headline states, "MARCO A RUSSO HAS PROTEST WITH THE BOARD OF ALDERMAN THE GRANTING OF LICENCE TO MUENCHINGER KING AND VIKING BECAUSE ARE LOCATED IN 200 FEET OF MT. ZION CHURCH."[61] The dispute and negativity weigh heavily on the newspaper, as the quality of articles and editorials become increasingly poor. The pettiness continues into 1937, and the headlines on the front

---

the United States.), etc. Also Russo's list of questions and answers are taken directly from the Citizenship Test. In the left column the questions and answers are written in English, while in the right column appears the corresponding information in Italian. In the following examples D. refers to the word in Italian for question (domanda), and R. refers to answer (risposta). D. Have you read the Constitution of the United States? R. Yes. / D. Avete letto la Costituzione degli Stati Uniti? R. Si' [sic]. D. What form of Government is this? R. Republican / D. Scito che forma di Governo siamo? R. Repubblicano. D. Who makes the laws of the United States? R. The Congress / D. Chi fa le leggi per gli Stati Uniti? R. Il Congresso., etc.

[59] See *The Newport Mercury and Weekly News*, Friday, June 19, 1936, page 7.
[60] See *L'Alba*, Saturday, July 11, 1936, Front Page.
[61] See *L'Alba*, Saturday, November 21, 1936, Front Page.

page of the May 29, 1937 edition announce, "RUSSO DECLARES MAYOR AND ALDERMAN JOHN MAHAN UNFIT TO HOLD OFFICE."[62] Russo seemed to be totally obsessed with his disagreement with the aldermen and the mayor to the point that *L'Alba* was suffering, and he was unable to focus on repairing the damage and improving his paper. August 14, 1937 seems to be the final issue of *L'Alba*. There is no farewell to his readers, no message or gesture of appreciation, merely a final headline taking a potshot at the mayor. This sad ending to a newspaper which enjoyed an auspicious beginning and ran quite successfully for more than three decades is truly unfortunate.

The Italian Review

The Italian Review was a brief enterprise which introduced Alexander Bevilacqua to the community of Rhode Island journalists. His first issue of this eight-page, Italo-American newspaper, written entirely in English, was distributed on March 29, 1926. A single copy cost three cents, and a one-year subscription could be purchased for two dollars. The paper reported news of Italy, the United States, and Rhode Island. In Volume One, Number One, the front page displayed two articles, two advertisements, a feature called "Melting Pot," and an index of the edition. Beside the "Melting Pot," which was a column of general interest and fun facts, the newspaper also included a feature called "Society," which reported birthdays, weddings, engagements, as well as, banquets and receptions of area organizations. An editorial page, a sports page, and a feature entitled "Tidbits" — a column of short blurbs of general interest about Providence and Rhode Island — completed *The Italian Review*. The staff, housed at 50 South Water St., Providence, RI, consisted of Alexander

---

[62] *L'Alba*, Saturday, May 29, 1937, Front Page.

Bevilacqua as editor, Edward Bevilacqua, Business Manager, Robert Gonnella, Circulation Manager, and Miss Marie Masso, Society Editor. In its first year the paper, described as " a weekly newspaper of free expression for people of Italian nativity and extraction," was extremely well received by the Italian community in Rhode Island.

In January of 1925 the paper moved its office to 277 Atwells Avenue in Providence. It added a crossword puzzle, and a novelette series entitled, "Sinners in Heaven," written by English author Clive Arden, and sold at five cents per copy. The May 9, 1925 edition of *The Italian Review* noted a change in the management of the paper. Thomas S. Luongo, proprietor of The Review Press, was now listed as publisher, while Alexander Bevilacqua continued as editor. In October of 1925, however, Bevilacqua is no longer with the paper, and Luongo was listed as editor. In that month the newspaper added an Italian section on page five, written by Vincenzo E. Cinquegrana, but by December of the same year, things looked grim. *The Italian Review* published its final issue on December 19, 1925.

The Rhode Island Italo-American

Ubaldo U. M. Pesaturo was a journalist and author of two books about Italian Americans in Rhode Island. His first book was published in 1936 under the title *Italo-Americans of Rhode Island: Their Contributions and Achievements.* His second book, entitled, *Italo-Americans of Rhode Island: An Historical and Biographical Survey of the Origin, Rise, and Progress of Rhode Islanders of Italian Birth or Descent* was issued in 1940. Pesaturo also wrote several articles about the Rhode Island Italo-American community for *The Providence Journal,* which were very well received. Following this success, Pesaturo resolved to publish a newspaper for the Italian Americans of Rhode Island. His first attempt, *The Rhode Island Italo-American,* issued on October 12, 1938, "written on the occasion of the Columbus Day Anniversary," [63] listed Ubaldo U. M. Pesaturo, editor and proprietor. This issue consists of eight pages in English and appears to be a history of the Italian American Community in Rhode Island, as well as, of the Aurora Club, and the Italo-American Club of Rhode Island. A second edition was never produced; however, on Sunday, October 12, 1941, he began to publish a ten-page newspaper under the title, *Americans All!*, which is written entirely in English, except for one column entitled "L'uomo Colombo" (The Man Columbus). The endeavor was also short lived, and there is no record as to how long the paper was in print. The Rhode Island Historical Society houses the only remaining copy of *Americans All!* at their research library in Providence, along with the only copy of *The Rhode Island Italo-American*.

Italia USA

In 1993 a group of Rhode Island businessmen and entrepreneurs formed a publishing company which they called Italia U.S.A. Publishing Inc., with the intention of producing a newspaper for the Rhode Island Italian American community. After much planning and collaboration on June 15, 1993 a new Italian American newspaper, in addition to *The Echo*, was distributed to the Rhode Island Italo-American community. The title of the newspaper was *Italia USA*, written mostly in English with several bilingual pages of news and information written in Italian and English. The front page of the paper was unique as it was printed in color. The header consisted of two thin red and green lines, between which, in tiny italic print, was written "The Area's Finest Italo/American Newspaper." Below the green line, in large black italic print, the words, Italia U.S.A., appear. Between the words Italia and U.S.A. is an oblong silhouette of a globe. This title sat above two thin red and blue lines between which, the volume and issue

---

[63] *The Rhode Island Italo-American*, Vol. 1, Number 1. Page 1.

number (to the far left), the name of the publishing company (in the center), and the date (to the far right) is written. Running down the left-hand margin of the front page, beneath the subtitle "What's Inside," is a series of multi-color boxes which listed the main features of the newspaper and their page numbers. The color of the front page gives the paper an impressive, and eye-catching appearance. *Italia U.S.A.*, a bi-monthly publication, was priced at fifty cents per copy, or subscribers could purchase the paper for twenty dollars per year, (fifteen dollars for senior citizens).

In Volume 1, Number 1 the headline read "Extra! Extra! New Italian Newspaper Hits the Streets..." In this front-page story, the readers are introduced to the publishers and editors of *Italia U.S.A.*, several of whom were very familiar to the readership, as they had previously written for *The Echo* during the Baccari era. Photographs of publisher and staff writer Arnold Abatecola, editor Joe Fuoco, Michael Di Chiro, Robert Antignano, and managing editor Michael J. Nunes all appear alongside a brief biography of each man. The second front page story, on the right-hand column is entitled "The Great Feasts and Festivals of Summer," and is accompanied by a photograph of the statue of St. Rocco, and one of St. Bartholomew. "We are new, we are fresh, not brash, but confident. We are beholden to none but the Italian American, and we exist as a newspaper to foster the Italian American ethos"[64] opens a commentary, written by Joe Fuoco, entitled "The Mission of Italia U.S.A." on the editorial page, found on page twenty-two of the paper. In his commentary Fuoco celebrates the "Italian contribution to western civilization," as he describes the mission of the new newspaper. He continues, "We are dedicated to the ex-

---

[64] *Italia U.S.A.*, Volume 1, Number 1, page 22.

ploration of the Italian American ethos in all its facets, in every field of human endeavor."[65]

Having established the mission of the paper, *Italia U.S.A.* offered distinct features to their readers. "Arnaldo's Italy" was a bilingual column recounting the history of Italy, and "Buongiorno" was a general interest column focusing on Rhode Island and Italian American Rhode Islanders. The paper also offered a travel section, a movie review section, and a sports section. "Colore Locale" was a feature which provided readers information about upcoming banquets, conventions, festivals, and award ceremonies in and around the state. The newspaper also offered several informational columns such as "Mangia with Marge," a food and recipe column written by Marge Caprara. "Beva with Lombard," written by Lombard Gasbarro, discussed Italian wines, and the wine regions of Italy. Joe Fuoco offered a column in which he wrote about the Italian Neighborhoods of Rhode Island entitled "Joe's Corner," and for each issue of the paper the staff would choose a Rhode Island family which they would showcase in a column entitled "Tempi Belli."

Italia U.S.A. was truly a Rhode Island centered newspaper, and the editors and staff strove to underscore the importance of the Italian American community in the state. Attorney Michael Di Chiro, one of the founders of the paper, explains that the impetus for publishing *Italia U.S.A.* was "to preserve the Italian culture in Rhode Island."[66]

Italia U.S.A. was printed as a bi-monthly newspaper from June 1993 until December 1994. In January of 1995 the paper changed to a monthly publication but continued to provide the quality and in-depth content which attracted its readers. The front page of the first issue of 1995, Volume

---

[65] Ibid.
[66] This quote is taken from a phone interview between the author and Michael Di Chiro.

3, #1, dated January 20, 1995, featured a tribute to Claude Campellone (who is the subject of Chapter 4), by his daughter Marian. Beneath Marian Campellone's tribute to her father, an address from the president of Italy, Oscar Luigi Scalfaro appears, entitled, "Il messaggio di fine anno del presidente della repubblica, Oscar Luigi Scalfaro." Inside this issue readers enjoyed a *Cruciverbo* (a crossword puzzle in Italian), an article by Angelo Bianchi entitled, "I am an Italian American," a news page written in Italian, and a new feature entitled, "I Grandi Maestri" written by Lawrence Izzi. This new feature began with this edition of the paper, and occupied pages eleven and twelve, the focus of which was the famous medieval Italian author, Dante Alighieri. Finally, on page fifteen, the reader finds in depth coverage of the inauguration of Lincoln Almond, Rhode Island's 56th governor.

In February of 1996 the editors of *Italia U.S.A.* surveyed their readers to ascertain how they could improve the newspaper. Results found that readers overwhelmingly wanted the paper to return to a bi-monthly publication, and in April of 1996, *Italia U.S.A.* was once again printed twice a month. While the paper continued to be a strong presence in the Rhode Island Italo-American community, by midyear of 1998 trouble seemed to be on the horizon. By the end of 1997 *Italia U.S.A.* had returned to a monthly format, and by December of 1998 the newspaper seemed to be struggling. Volume 7 #2, dated March/April 1999 was the final issue of *Italia U.S.A.*, and on the front page the editors bade farewell to their faithful readers. In an emotional front-page editorial, entitled "Another Italian-American Newspaper to Fade into History" Arnaldo Abatecola writes, "We have tried our best, and still think that *Italia U.S.A.* was worth the effort for our Italian American community. We thought the paper could have been the glue that would keep together the hundreds of Italo-American Clubs and Societies in the area, evidently this has not worked...We tried very hard and have no regrets. We appreciate that we were able to make a small contribution to our wonderful culture. Best wishes to all of you."

The Federal Hill Gazette

Two years after the first issue of *Italia U.S.A.*, and before Robert D'Uva revived *The Rhode Island Echo*, a young entrepreneur from Providence named Robert L. Salvatore, assembled a team to help him create a newspaper specific to the Federal Hill neighborhood of Providence. On September 14, 1995, Volume 1, Number 1 of the *Federal Hill Gazette* debuted. With an office at 55 Bradford Street in Providence, the paper was produced in the heart of the Federal Hill neighborhood. President & Publisher Robert L. Salvatore, and Editor in Chief Joe Fuoco are listed as staff. The paper lists Mayor Vincent A. Cianci, State Representative Steven Constantino, and City Councilman John J. Lombardi as contributing members. Consisting of eighteen pages, the front page of the premier issue of the *Federal Hill Gazette* features a profile drawing of Joe Fuoco, beneath the title. The title *Federal Hill Gazette* is written in large block letters in black ink. Beneath the moniker, on the left, an image of the capital of an Ionic column appears, much like the columns that flank the arch on Atwells Avenue in Providence. To the far right, in quotes the words "Where Good Food and Good Friends Meet." are included. On page two, an editorial written by Joe Fuoco occupies the top quarter of the page. Entitled "This is the Hill," Fuoco's editorial waxes nostalgic, as well as provides a brief history about this very popular Rhode Island neighborhood. The opening paragraph reads, "Federal Hill is the crucible. It is and has always been the forging place, the place where dreams were born, and monuments built. It is the merging place, and it is where the dispossessed, the ambitious, and the dreamers have always come." This paragraph became the statement of identity for the paper, and it appears on the editorial page of every issue of the *Federal Hill Gazette*. On page three of Volume 1, Number 1 appeared an article written, again by Joe Fuoco, entitled "The Federal Hill Story from Roots to Revival, Part 1." Page four carries three political columns written by the aforementioned politicians. Page seven includes a food section called "Great Tastes," and a crossword puzzle. Features on arts and entertainment, antiques and collectibles, and sports could be found on pages nine through fifteen. While the paper was free per copy, the publisher offered a one-year subscription for $29.99. For the initial four months the *Federal Hill Gazette* was printed bi-monthly, however, beginning with the January 1996 issue, the paper became a monthly publication. The staff increased the number of pages of the paper, and in February added a personal ad section which included a 1-900 number, which readers could call and leave messages for ads, as well as listen to recorded greetings. The *Federal Hill Gazette* proved to be a very successful newspaper, and in January of 1997 once again increased in size to a forty page paper. Many columns of general interest were added to the paper such as a genealogy column, and sections on travel, real estate, recreation, and book reviews. Along the bottom of the Front Page of the January 1997 issue ran the announcement of a webpage; "See us in [sic] the internet: www.FedHillGazette.com." Volume 4, Number 1 (January 1998) presented a facelift to the front page, as the title (still in black ink) appears on a green field enclosed in a red rectangle whose top center is a half-circle that accommodates the H,L,L, of the word Hill. The paper also had a distinct political flavor as many of Rhode Island's political dignitaries wrote columns for the paper. Along with the mayor's column Salvatore added a space for the Governor Lincoln Almond, U.S. Representative Patrick Kennedy, and U. S. Senator Jack Reed. Robert Salvatore's newspaper was thriving and became one of Rhode Island's most popular monthly publications.

While enjoying success well into the new century, a series of changes began to occur to the publication in July of 2002. With this issue the publisher is listed as Renaissance Communications, and the editor is Linda Parentau. Beneath the list of staff, "Robert L. Salvatore-Founder " appears. Parentau served as editor until September 2002, at which time, Rhode Island attorney Marc Press took control of the paper, and the *Federal Hill Gazette* continued to be a premier newspaper in the state. Replacing several of the original columns, new sections were added in July of 2006. A restaurant guide entitled "Buon Appetito," a gardening question and answer column, a financial advice column, a recipe and food column called "Si Cucina Bene," and a personal advice column all graced the *Federal Hill Gazette*. Marc Press brought the popular Rhode Island chef, Walter Potenza on staff to provide readers a column about the regions of Italy and their cuisine. Each month Potenza wrote about historical and geographical information of the regions and included a typical recipe of that region. Potenza's column quickly became extremely popular with the readers of the paper. Local mortician Robert Nardolillo Jr. provided a column on death and bereavement, in which he offered information and advice regarding bereavement and funeral planning.

January of 2007 signaled more changes for the *Federal Hill Gazette*. Marc Press and Robert D'Uva, are listed as publishers with Deb Dellasanta as managing editor. In one section, half of the paper, immediately following Nardolillo's column, the staff added a page of prayers and novenas to the Madonna, St. Jude, and St. Claire. A new website was also launched with this issue. The paper could now be read at www.thefederalhillgazette.net. Volume 13, Number 12 (December 2007) seems to be the final issue of the *Federal Hill Gazette*. The paper consisted of fifty-six pages, with the headlines on the front page announcing Bright Night 2008. All the columns ran as usual, however, there was never a printed copy after December 2007. The *Federal Hill Gazette* became a total web-based newspaper, which endured for an additional eight years, until September of 2016. Not as in-depth as the paper copy, the web-based newspaper continued to run many of its regular columns, and stories of interest, including "The Italian Page," which was a bilingual page offering information about Italian culture, written by Daniela Ciccone and Lou Turchetta. Interested readers are still able to access issues from January 2013 to September 2016 at www.thefederalhillgazette.com. By March 2015 content on the website had begun to dwindle, although the staff made a great effort to continue to provide a quality web-based newspaper. The July 2016 issue, however, contains only three items; there is no August issue, and the September 2016 issue consists of only a thirty second video of a dog named Moses posing on an unidentified beach with a spectacular rainbow in the background. For twenty-one years, in print and combined with its web-based newspaper, the *Federal Hill Gazette* provided news, information, and entertainment to its readers, thereby adding its title to the list of distinguished newspapers which served the Italian American community of Rhode Island.

PART TWO

FROM PRINT TO THE AIRWAVES

Chapter Three

ANTONIO PACE AND *THE ITALO-AMERICAN RADIO REVIEW*

> *Pace exudes charm and poise. He shows, too,*
> *that he appreciates the magic of the human*
> *touch and its value in business, as well as in art*
> *or entertainment.*
>
> The Providence Journal

A little-known cheese and olive oil importer took great pride in providing the food and culture of Italy to the Italian community of Rhode Island. Soon, however, he would be the central link between this community and relatives and friends in their *patria*. Much more than purveyor of food, Antonio Pace would become the pioneer who opened the airwaves to bring Italy into the homes of Rhode Island's Italo-Americans.

In August of 1935, the newspaper *The Italian Echo* reported that the popular Italian language radio program "Il Mattino e La Sera di New York," hosted by Luigi Di Fant, had begun broadcasting in Providence to great success. The paper reported that "so great has been the response that its sponsors are considering a twice a day broadcast,"[67] which, in fact, came to fruition two weeks later. The 9:45 a.m. program became extremely popular, among the Rhode Island Italian immigrants, who found listening to the latest news from Italy in their native tongue a source of both comfort and pride. "È veramente sorprendente il successo del signor Di Fant e noi, interpreti del sentimento popolare, gli inviamo sentite congratulazioni e sinceri ringraziamenti per il conforto spirituale

---

[67] *L'Eco di Rhode Island*, Friday, August 30, 1935, Editorial Page.

ch'egli apporta alle famiglie italiane,"[68] wrote the editor of *The Italian Echo*, Antonio Pace. At the end of 1935, Di Fant hired Pace as an announcer for the program on WPRO in Providence, and within two months, Pace bought the program and produced his own home-grown Italian radio program for friends and neighbors in Rhode Island. *The Italo-American Radio Review*, a weekly program broadcast in Italian on WPRO, which later moved to WFCI in Pawtucket, was the beginning of a long and distinguished radio career for Antonio Pace.

On May 9, 1898, Antonio Pace was born in Ortona a Mare, in the Abruzzo region of Italy. He attended the Italian Royal Naval Academy in Livorno and served for five years as a lieutenant. On a transatlantic voyage with the Italian Navy in 1921, Pace arrived at the Port of Providence. While in the city, he dined at the home of Nicola DiDomenico and was introduced to DiDomenico's daughter Irma who soon became the object of Pace's affection. His commission in the Italian Navy, however, soon returned him to Italy, and onto other ocean adventures. One such voyage brought Pace to Nova Scotia where his ship docked in the port of Halifax. By chance, Edward, the Prince of Wales, (later to become King Edward VIII, until his abdication of the throne in 1936) who had been touring North America was also in Halifax. Prince Edward's ship was docked next to the Italian naval vessel, and as was the Prince's custom, he boarded the Italian ship to pay a courtesy visit to the Italian sailors. Having earned very high grades in English class, Antonio Pace was appointed ship's interpreter to facilitate communication between the Prince of Wales and the Command of the Italian Royal Navy.

---

[68] Ibid. "The success of Mr. Di Fant is truly surprising, and we, interpreters of popular sentiment, send him our heartfelt congratulations and sincere thanks for the spiritual comfort which he brings to the Italian families."

Upon completing his service in the Italian Royal Navy, Pace embarked on an exciting new transatlantic adventure. On March 14, 1923, Antonio Pace emigrated from his beloved town of Ortona a Mare to begin a new life in America. Upon his arrival in Providence, Pace visited Irma DiDomenico at her parents' home. This was the beginning of their courtship which culminated in their wedding at Holy Ghost Church on April 15, 1925. Irma and Antonio had three children. Their first son Rocco was born in December of 1926. At the age of thirteen, however, the boy succumbed to an illness and died in February of 1940. Harold, the Pace's second son, was born in October of 1928. Harold enjoyed a very distinguished career as Chief of Protocol at the U.S. Department of State in Washington, D.C. He also served as General Manager of his father's radio station, WRIB from 1958 through 1962. Irma and Antonio's daughter Maria, born in September of 1943, taught French and Italian at Lincoln High School, in Lincoln, Rhode Island.

As Pace began to produce his own radio program on WPRO in 1935, his show quickly became quite popular among the Italo-Americans of Rhode Island. One of the most popular features from that early program was entitled "the Mystery Voice," in which Pace would play a voice recording of a community member, and listeners would try to identify the voice. In his memoirs, Pace states, "It was a tremendous audience builder and those who advertised on my program had more business than they could handle."[69] As Pace's program gained popularity, so did his notoriety, and he was soon hired by a Pawtucket newspaper entitled *The Tribune* as their special correspondent in Italy. During one of his many trips to Italy, Pace was contacted by Benito Mussolini's Director of Radio Propaganda, and invited to speak on Radio 2-RO, an international Italian

---

[69] *The Echo*, September 25, 1970.

radio network which was broadcast in that era. Pace recounts that following that evening's broadcast, as he and his wife entered the dining room at their hotel, "everyone rose and gave me the fascist salute, raising their right arms high." Reflecting on the scene in his memoirs Pace writes, "This episode has always remained vivid in my mind. It is an excellent example of the servile attitude of a people subject to a dictatorship; always ready to pay homage to their oppressors."[70]

It was during this time that Antonio Pace planned to implement an idea which he believed would greatly enhance his radio program. His plan was to travel to the villages and towns from which Rhode Islanders had emigrated to record the voices of their relatives. Upon returning to Providence, he planned to play the recordings on his radio show so that the Italians in Rhode Island could hear their relatives and family members from their respective *paesi*. Having obtained a letter from the Italian Ambassador in Washington, permitting Pace to enter Italy with his "large, bulky, and very heavy"[71] recording equipment, he traveled by ship to France. Upon his arrival he boarded a train to Paris, and then another to Modane, an Italian border town. At the border, Pace presented the ambassador's letter to the Chief Inspector who was immediately suspicious and uncertain that recording equipment from another country was allowed in Italy. Pace's equipment was confiscated, and an armed customs agent accompanied him from Modane to Torino. In Torino, he was shuttled from one inspector to the next until he was directed to speak to the Director of Customs who explained the matter had to go to Rome. In Rome, Antonio met with a high customs official named Commendatore Page who apologized for the inconvenience and explained that the proper

---

[70] *The Echo*, September 25, 1970.
[71] *The Echo*, October 2, 1970.

permits would be issued the following day. For five days the excuses continued, until finally Antonio was told the permits would not be issued. Pace, along with his equipment, was returned to the United States, and his recording project was put on hold until after World War II.

During the war, Pace's program was placed under strict surveillance by the FBI. A monitor assigned to Pace would read transcripts of the program the night before airtime. By 1941, Pace's program had moved to WFCI in Pawtucket, Rhode Island, and his news broadcasts were a literal translation of the news which was provided by the International News Service and the United Press. Pace received regular visits from two FBI agents who often interrogated him in an effort to gain information on potential Facist sympathizers within the Italian American community. As the sole Italian broadcaster on the air in Rhode Island during World War II, Pace provided essential news and information to the Italian diaspora of Providence and Rhode Island as a whole. "Thousands of families who had children and fathers in the war depended on my program for war information," wrote Pace.[72] In his memoirs, Pace also remembers the heart-breaking tasks of reporting on air the news of bombardments of Italian villages and towns where family and friends were in constant danger. "I knew Italy well and I knew the places that were being destroyed, especially my hometown of Ortona, where the front stopped for over two months. My family was living in Ortona, and my heart would ache when I gave news stories on the battles going on in the town," remembers Pace.[73]

In 1946, collaborating with Judge Harold Acaro, William Considine, and former Democratic state chairman, Frank Rao, Pace established the WRIB radio station at

---

[72] *The Echo*, January 8, 1971
[73] Ibid.

1220 on the AM dial, with a format centered on foreign language programming. In his book, *Immigration, Diversity, and Broadcasting in the United States*, Vibert Cambridge states,

> "Since the introduction of broadcasting in the United States in the early 1920s, immigrants and native born minority groups...have been providing news and information from their home countries and about their present communities, transmitting their cultural heritage, orienting their audiences to the American way of life, encouraging participation in the political and economic life of their new communities, providing entertainment, and overcoming stereotypes."[74]

While Antonio Pace and his *Italo-American Radio Review* provided all these services to the Italian American community of Providence and surrounding cities, his station also featured programs in Spanish, Portuguese, Polish, Greek, and Armenian. Licenced as a "daytime radio station," WRIB had limited airtime from sunrise to sunset. Each day the station would sign off the air at the official time of sunset.

Daily announcements of the most recent births and deaths in the Rhode Island Italian community was another valued feature of Pace's program. Later, in the 1950s, Pace augmented his already popular radio show with the broadcast of Italian soap operas which entertained and delighted Rhode Island's Italo-American community. It was during these years that Pace was finally able to implement his plan (which had been derailed by the Fascists) to record diverse sounds of Italian life. He would travel to Italy where he would record village church bells, sounds in

---

[74] See Cambridge, Vibert. *Immigration, Diversity, and Broadcasting in the United States, 1900–2001*. Ohio: Ohio University Press, 2005.

a piazza, activity inside an Italian store, or banter at a local *caffè*. The feature, however, most anticipated by Rhode Island Italians each week was the voice recordings of their relatives. During each trip to Italy, Pace would visit specific villages such as Cassino, Ortona, Caserta, Frosinone, Pontecorvo, and many others from which the Italians in Rhode Island had emigrated. Each town in which he arrived gave him a hero's welcome. On many occasions, the village band would play as hundreds of people greeted him in the main piazza. As Pace recounts, "[T]hey were all clutching little pieces of paper in their hands on which was written the greeting they were to record for their relatives in Rhode Island.[75] In 1954, Kenneth W. Parker wrote an article for the *Providence Journal*, entitled "WRIB's Antonio Pace." Parker reported that Pace "goes to Italy two or three times a year to interview relatives of Rhode Islanders, tape-recording their voices and bringing them back to be played on his three-hour show."[76] Pace explained to Parker that he would visit *paesi* "within 100 miles of Cassino all around ... ninety per cent [sic] of the families have relatives here." Thus Pace, through the simple act of recording these relatives' voices, would reunite the distant family members and bring great joy and comfort to the entire Italian diaspora of Rhode Island and southern Massachusetts.

In the early 1960s, immediately following Pace's *Italo-American Radio Review*, a news and commentary program aired hosted by Luigi Scala. Scala, a Sicilian immigrant, was the president of the Columbus National Bank until his retirement in 1967. Pace and Scala were close friends, and Pace recognized the essential contribution Scala could make to the programming at WRIB and thus invited him to produce a news program for the station. Presented in a bilingual format, Scala reported the latest news from Italy,

---

[75] *The Echo*, February 5, 1971.
[76] *Providence Journal*, December 29, 1954, p. 10.

the U.S.A., and Rhode Island, in both English and Italian. The Italo-Americans of the state came to depend on Scala's news program as well as the commentary and interpretation which he provided. Scala's program became so popular that it was picked up by WHIM 1110 AM.

While Antonio Pace is best known as a popular radio personality, his fund-raising acumen and generosity were also fundamental elements of his legacy. He and his wife, Irma, raised thousands of dollars which were distributed on several different occasions to relief projects in Italy. After arriving in the United States, Pace worked as an importer of Italian cheeses and wines. Later, while he was producing his radio program at WFCI, he also taught physics at Samuel Bridgham Jr. High School in Providence. He had always credited his success in fund-raising to his business and teaching experiences. One of his earliest projects was in 1946 in which he and Irma raised 200,000 lire ($700.00) from the Italo-Americans of Rhode Island. Pace personally delivered this charity to the "poor and sick of his war-torn native town of Ortona."[77] *The Providence Journal* praised Pace in a *front-page* article calling him the "Providence Ambassador of Mercy."[78] Antonio and Irma also raised funds to benefit Italian children mutilated during World War II, victims of the Po Valley floods in 1952, and Irma's personal project, a campaign to raise funds to assist Radio Free Europe. In his memoirs, Pace refers to his wife Irma as "the sole inspiration of anything good and honest that I performed in the many years as a radio broadcaster when the Italo-American Radio Review...became the champion of human need and suffering."[79] In 1955, Pope Pius XII awarded Irma the distinguished service medal, "Pro Ecclesia et

---

[77] *Providence Journal*, December 6, 1946, p. 1.

[78] Ibid.

[79] *The Echo*, September 18, 1970.

Pontifice," for her "unswerving dedication to the spirit of Christian charity."[80]

Always cognizant of imposing upon the generosity of the Italian American community, Antonio Pace sought alternative methods of fund-raising to respond to the "continuous appeals from Italy"[81] which he received. One of these methods was a pseudo-documentary of war-ravaged Italian towns, filmed by Pace and his son Harold. Father and son traveled to Italy where, for two weeks, they photographed and filmed thirty towns. Upon their return, Pace and Harold presented their film *I Nostri Paesi* ("*Our Towns*") in theaters throughout Rhode Island, Southern Massachusetts, and Eastern Connecticut. The film was not only well-received but also a successful vehicle for fund-raising that benefitted multiple charitable organizations and relief efforts.

In the early 1960s, Antonio Pace's nephew Nick Ruggieri, Jr. was hired as a radio announcer for the Saturday program, as well as times when Antonio Pace was traveling. Ruggieri's most vivid memory dates back to November 23, 1963, while filling in for his uncle who was in Italy, when he "with great difficulty attempted to report the details of the Kennedy assassination in Italian without a script."[82] Ruggieri was with WRIB for several years until, having been hired at the Department of State, he moved to Washington, D.C.

During another trip to Rome in 1966, Irma Pace became very ill, requiring the couple to return to America. As the year progressed, so did Irma's illness, and on October 28, 1966, she died peacefully in the arms of her loving Antonio. Devastated by the untimely death of his wife, Pace decided to sell WRIB and retire from broadcasting.

---

[80] Ibid.
[81] *The Echo*, June 11, 1971.
[82] Interview with Nick Ruggieri, Jr.

The sale of WRIB to The Springfield Broadcasting Company[83] in early 1967 marked the end of Antonio Pace's radio broadcasting career. Remaining very active in the Italo-American community of Rhode Island, Pace continued to promote Italian culture and to serve the Italian Americans of the state. As chronicled in Chapter One, Pace and his son Harold, in March of 1970, revived *The Echo* to one of Rhode Island's foremost ethnic newspaper and remained with the paper until January of 1972.

Antonio Pace married Mary Fabiano in 1970, and the couple lived a joyful life together until Antonio's death on August 8, 1977. Among the accolades conferred upon him by the Italian government were Cavaliere del Lavoro in 1950, for his service to the Italian people, and in 1952, the Stella della Solidarietà Italiana (Star of Italian Solidarity), for his and Irma's relief efforts on behalf of the victims of the flood of the Po Valley. Pace also served as the president of the Federation of Italian War Veterans. Whether at the microphone, making audio recordings in Italy, raising funds for charity, or publishing a newspaper, Antonio Pace continuously promoted Italian culture and served Rhode Island's Italian community. To this day, Pace is fondly remembered by older Rhode Islanders who faithfully listened to his radio program as the pioneer who, each week, brought Italy into Rhode Island homes.

---

[83] July 7, 2006, WRIB (1220 AM) was purchased by Faith Christian Center, which abruptly ended all foreign language programming, and the station went silent. (Allaccess.com). On November 29, 2017, the station returned to the air with the call letters WSTL broadcasting Hispanic music.

Chapter Four

CLAUDIO CAMPELLONE AND *LA FESTA ITALIANA*

> *Claude L. Campellone was one of those*
> *protagonists who was a true pillar in the*
> *Italian-American community.*
>
> Marian (Campellone) Martin

A new Italian radio program filled the air waves in Rhode Island in 1954, and at the microphone sat Claudio L. Campellone, who produced and directed the program. Campellone, a teacher of French in the Cranston Public School District, purchased airtime on WRIB and hosted a half-hour music program immediately following Antonio Pace's *Italo American Radio Review.* The format of Campellone's show differed from Pace's pro-gram in that it was primarily for entertainment, showcasing the latest musical artists and hits from Italy.

Born on January 7, 1913, in Colli al Volturno in the Campobasso province of Italy, Campellone received his high school diploma from the Instituto Guicciardini. At the age of seventeen, he boarded the steamship *Augustus,* landing at Ellis Island on August 19, 1930. Upon arriving in Rhode Island, he enrolled at Providence College, where he earned a Bachelor of Arts degree. With his strong in-tellect and great enthusiasm for education, Campellone spent the next two years at Boston University School of Law. He enlisted in the United States Air Force in 1941 and quickly earned the rank of lieutenant. During World War II, his deployment began in Algiers, then subse-quently he was sent to the European theatre where he served in Italy, France, Germany, and finally, Austria. One afternoon, following the liberation of Paris, while Campellone patrolled the streets of the city, he came upon a beautiful French *mademoiselle* whose bicycle tire had gone flat. The dashing American soldier stopped his Jeep and offered to help the young lady. Having repaired the tire, the soldier bid farewell to the French lass; however, a spark between the two had been ignited, and they continued to correspond through the remainder of the war. After the war, having completed his service to the Air Force, Campellone returned to Paris where he enrolled in the Sorbonne, to pursue a degree in French literature. While in Paris, he visited and courted Jeanne Garraud (his bicycle sweetheart). The two fell in love and were married at the Cathedral of *Notre Dame* in Paris. Soon Jeanne was with child, and upon Campellone's completion of his degree at the Sorbonne, the couple decided to return to the United States. In 1953, Claudio and Jeanne boarded the ocean-liner *La Liberté* at the port of Le Havre, France. Halfway across the ocean, Jeanne's time came due, and she gave birth to a son John, whose place of birth is officially recorded as "International Waters." The Campellone family arrived in New York on July 22, 1953. Once settled in Rhode Island, Campellone accepted a position in the Cranston School Department teaching French at Cranston High School. It was at this time that Claudio Campellone began his radio career. Several years later, the Campellones were blessed with a daughter Marian who, following her father's death, would continue to produce his radio program.

Antonio Pace and Claudio Campellone had both served as editors of *The Echo* newspaper. Pace held Campellone in great esteem, and in January of 1954, Pace invited Campellone to broadcast several shows on WRIB. Soon, Campellone, assisted by Virgilio De Vecchis, the founder of the Italian American Historical Society of Rhode Island, was producing his own show entitled *La Festa Italiana*. The show became extremely popular with listeners, and in 1961,

Campellone moved the program to WWRI at 1450 kHz in West Warwick, Rhode Island. *La Festa Italiana* was a weekly musical variety program which featured traditional and pop music from Italy. Artists such as Claudio Villa, Domenico Modugno, Betty Curtis, Massimo Ranieri, Mina, Gianni Morandi, and many others filled the Rhode Island airwaves on Campellone's program. Listeners tuned in every Sunday morning from 10:00 a.m. until 12:00 p.m. to hear the music of Italy, as well as news and announcements pertaining to the Italian American community of Rhode Island. As Campellone's program quickly gained popularity, he began to attract sponsors from around the state. Many local businesses, such as Pastene, Supreme Dairy, Tops Electric, and Carcieri's Market, sought to advertise during the broadcasts of *La Festa Italiana*. The advertisements for local businesses were written and announced in Italian by Campellone; however, the program also promoted imported Italian products such as Brioschi Effervescent Antacid, with professionally produced ads.

In 1969, Judge Harold Arcaro encouraged Campellone to relocate his radio show to WHIM 1110 on the AM dial, where Arcaro was president of the station. Enjoying great success, Campellone spent the next ten years at WHIM, until 1980, when the station abandoned its special programming and established a total Country & Western format.[84] The Sunday morning programing which included not only *La Festa Italiana*, but also Armenian, Polish, and Portuguese programs, was cancelled. Claudio Campellone was once again in search of a home for his radio show, which he found at 550 kHz, WGNG in Pawtucket, Rhode Island. His show aired every Sunday night from 6:00p.m. to 8:00 p.m., where he remained until December of 1986. The Roger Williams Broadcasting Corporation sold WGNG in

---

[84] See *Broadcasting Yearbook 1980*, p. C-201

1985 to Beam Communications Inc.[85] While remaining at 550 AM, the new owners changed the call letters to WICE and continued with the special Sunday programing, includeing *La Festa Italiana*, until the end of the year.

Returning to West Warwick, Campellone, along with his music engineer Peter Gallo, reestablished his program at 1450 AM WKRI. WKRI would become the permanent home of *La Festa Italiana*, as Campellone broadcasted from this station until his death in 1995.[86] Beginning in 1987, *La Festa Italiana* returned to Sunday mornings, from 9:00 a.m. until 12:00 p.m. It also enjoyed its longest period at any radio station in the program's history. Campellone's Italian radio program was extremely popular with his listeners, and advertisers alike. It was during this period that Claudio Campellone founded La Festa Italiana Society, a social organization comprised of many of his listeners from around the state, the goal of which was to preserve and promote Italian culture throughout Rhode Island. Along with benefits and fundraisers, La Festa Italiana Society sponsored an annual banquet which attracted hundreds of participants, among them listeners, local and national dignitaries, as well as fellow media personalities. The banquet raised thousands of dollars annually for local charities and disaster relief in Italy.[87]

---

[85] See *Broadcasting Yearbook 1985*, p. B-237, and *Broadcasting Yearbook 1986*, p. B-248

[86] Following Campellone's death, his daughter Marian continued to produce *La Festa Italiana* at 1450 AM. In 1996 DBH Broadcasting Inc. sold WKRI to the Providence Broadcasting Company, which changed the call sign to WHIM (See *Broadcasting & Cable Yearbook 1997*, p. B-394). While the official format of the station was Country & Western, it continued to broadcast *La Festa Italiana* on Sunday mornings. The show continued until 2002 at the same frequency, now under the call sign WLKW (See *Broadcasting & Cable Yearbook 2002/2003*, p. D-396) at which time the program was cancelled.

[87] The latest record I was able to find of La Festa Italiana Society is from a website reporting a $2000.00 donation to the National Multiple Sclerosis Society in August 2011. See https://pbn.com/festa-italiana-society-gives-support-to-ri-ms-society60627/. La Festa Italiana Society is presently defunct.

While the production and broadcasts of *La Festa Italiana* occupied much of Campellone's time, as he was no longer teaching, he also dedicated himself to his insurance and travel business, as well as various civic organizations. In 1970, he launched and served as president of an insurance agency under the name of Imperial Insurance. Several years later, Campellone inaugurated the Circolo Fratelli d'Italia, with its headquarters at 121 Ledge Street in the Marieville section of Providence. Similar to the Order of the Sons of Italy (l'Ordine dei Figli d'Italia), the mission of the Circolo was to preserve the Italian heritage through the teaching of the Italian language and the promotion of the Italian culture through music and art. An avid bocce player, Campellone was also a member of the St. Anthony Bocce League as well as a member of the Madonna dei Cipressi Society at St. Ann's Church in Providence. This Society was responsible for the annual festival in honor of the Virgin Mary under the title of Maria Santissima dei Cipressi, which originated in the village of Fontegreca, in the province of Caserta, Italy.

In 1977, Campellone renamed his insurance agency to Promote Travel and Insurance Agency and moved the business to Federal Hill. Campellone could often be found in his office on Dean Street in the Federal Hill section of Providence assisting his clients. Through his travel agency he often organized trips to Italy; more importantly, however, were the many services Campellone provided to the Italo-Americans of Rhode Island such as translation of official documents, notary services, and assistance with passport or pension applications. Many Italian immigrants of Rhode Island came to depend on the assistance of Campellone. In a memorial article published in *The Echo* in January of 1995, Virgilio De Vecchis describes Campellone as "a gentleman who spent many a long hour helping people and his community. He was a man who took it upon himself to help his fellow immigrants."[88] A humble man, who consistently put others before himself, Claudio Campellone kept above his desk a framed copy of the following quote:

> I expect to pass through this world but once. Any good, therefore, that I can do or any kindness that I can show to any fellow creature, let me do it now. For I shall not pass this way again.

Attributed to the Quaker missionary Stephen Grellet, these words capture the spirit of dedication which Campellone embodied, evidenced by the countless ways he assisted the Italian American community of Rhode Island.

Always striving to promote the Italian culture and connect the Italo-American community to their *patria*, in 1987, Campellone approached a local cable company, Dimension Cable, to convince the directors that Rhode Island needed a cable television station broadcast in the Italian language. The directors of Dimension Cable agreed to organize an exploratory committee with Claudio Campellone serving as its consultant. After many long hours of meetings and negotiations, Dimension Cable began broadcasting taped programing from the Italian state television network RAI. The Italian community of the state was overjoyed. Suddenly, they had access to television news, sitcoms, game shows, and soccer games from Italy, and they had Claudio Campellone to thank.

Campellone continued to produce and broadcast *La Festa Italiana* until December 1994. Each program opened with "Hai ragione cara mamma," sung by Italian pop artist Betty Curtis. At the end of each show, in the background listeners heard "Csárdás," played on accor-

---

[88] "In Memoriam Claudio L. Campellone," *The Echo,* January 13, 1995.

dion.[89] As Campellone gave the closing credits, he would sign off with, "La gioia più grande di vivere è la gioia che diamo agli altri;" ("The greatest joy in living is the joy we give others."). Claudio Campellone died on January 3, 1995, and in a tribute, *The Echo* newspaper wrote, "...just four days shy of his 82nd birthday, The Italian community lost one of its greatest champions and most prominent citizens."[90] Truly one of "the most prominent citizens" of Rhode Island's Italo-American community, Campellone will always be remembered for his devotion and dedication to the Italians of the state. In an interview, Claudio Campellone was quoted as saying, "I wanted to educate the Italian population and give them something that they could call their own."[91]

---

[89] "Csárdás" is a musical composition written by Italian composer Vittorio Monti, which is based on Hungarian folk music. The piece is traditionally played on violin or accordion. The following Youtube link showcases Rhode Island accordionist Cory Pesaturo in a live performance of Monti's "Czardas." https://www.youtube.com/watch?v=tw6p8n1unk0.
[90] See *The Echo*, January 13, 1995.
[91] "In Memoriam Claudio L. Campellone," *The Echo*, January 13, 1995.

Chapter Five

Rolando Petrella and *La Voce d'Italia*

*"Petrella served to link his native Italy
and his adopted Rhode Island through
his radio program."*

Providence Journal

As Rolando Petrella, leaving behind his wife, crossed
the Atlantic, little did he know that in a few short
years, he would become one of the most popular radio
personalities among the Italian American community of
Rhode Island.

Born in Caserta, Italy, on May 14, 1927, Petrella
attended the Liceo Salvatore Pizzi in Capua. After graduation, he trained for and served in the *Carabinieri*, Italy's
special police force unit. At the end of the Second World
War, Rolando Petrella, seeking adventure, decided to ride
his bike along the route which the American Army had
taken during the Allied liberation of Italy.

Beginning in his town of Caserta, Petrella rode north
toward Rome. On the outskirts of Rome, he discovered the
town of Guidonia Montecelio. A pleasant, picturesque
town, Petrella decided to remain there for some time.
Having rented a room, the young man set out to explore
Guidonia. In the *piazza* he met his landlord, the landlord's
daughter, and Paola Ruggieri, her best friend. Extremely
attractive, Paola caught Rolando's eye, and the handsome
gentleman from Caserta soon began to visit her at her
father's house. As Paola Petrella remembers, the two
began to have "very long conversations." Rolando would
stand in the *cortile* (courtyard), while the beautiful young
lady would speak to him from her window; "Proprio come
Romeo e Giuletta," (Just like Romeo and Juliette) adds

Paola. Several weeks passed, and it was soon time for Rolando to leave Guidonia, and report to training. He vowed to Paola that he would return in the splendid uniform of the *Carabinieri*. Each day Rolando wrote to his beloved. Paola, who admits that at first, she was not very impressed, found herself falling in love with her handsome suitor. One day there came a knock at the door. Opening the door, Paola found Rolando, dressed in the uniform of the Italian Special Police Force, on one knee proposing marriage. The couple was married on December 10, 1950.

In 1949, Petrella and a fellow *Carabiniere* were sent undercover to Sicily as part of the operation to apprehend the infamous Sicilian bandit Salvatore Giuliano. Disguised as traveling salesmen, the two government agents walked the towns of Sicily gathering information. One day, as they walked the streets, a black limousine rolled to a stop. Stepping out of the car, a man, who from their investigation they recognized as one of Giuliano's family members, approached them to ask what they were doing. Rolando explained that they were going door to door selling shirts and ties. Opening their valices, they proudly showed the man their wares. The gangster's cousin complimented the two undercover *carabinieri*, bought three ties from them, and wished them well in their career. Unfortunately, this is the closest encounter Petrella and his partner ever had with Salvatore Giuliano.

Arriving in New York on March 19, 1951, this former *Carabinere* who spoke no English found himself in a land where he knew no one. Petrella made his way to Providence, RI, where he immediately felt much more at home with the Italian community of Federal Hill. Taking menial jobs as a pants presser and a short order cook at Richard's Drive-In Restaurant in Warwick, he saved enough money to send for his wife and oldest son Gianpaolo to join him. The Petrella family grew over the years, adding four other children. Annamaria was born when Gianpaolo was two years old. In five more years Rita arrived, and then later Steven, and finally Roland, known as Dean.

In 1955, Petrella was introduced to Antonio Pace who invited the young protege to work at his radio station. While at WRIB, Pace noticed that Petrella possessed a talent at the microphone. He began to tutor Petrella, and before long, Italian Americans across the state were treated to the suave, supple voice of Rolando Petrella. By 1959, Petrella was producing his own radio program entitled *Piccolo Mondo* which aired on WWRI 1450 kHz in West Warwick, Rhode Island. *Piccolo Mondo* featured the latest pop music from Italy, bringing to the Rhode Island air- waves Italian hits such as "Tu vuò fà l'americano" sung by Renato Carosone, "Melodia d'amore" by Caterina Valent- e, "Napule ca se ne va" by Sergio Bruni, and "Tango italiano" by Milva. Always working to improve his program, Petrella added a feature to *Piccolo Mondo* that no other radio show could claim. The broadcast aired every Sunday from 1:00 p.m. to 3:00 p.m., and at the microphone, alongside his father, was ten-year-old Gianpaolo Petrella. Rolando billed the young disc jockey as "the world's young- est bilingual radio announcer," and Gianpaolo quickly be- came a great hit with Petrella's listeners. Spinning records, announcing local events for the Rhode Island Italian Ameri- can community, and answering the phone became second nature to Gianpaolo. Each Sunday featured a 15-minute segment, written and broadcast in English by Gianpaolo, which he called "We Are the Future." In October of 1961, the *Providence Sunday Journal* published an article about the young Petrella entitled "A Radio Pro at Age of 10," in which the author, Steve Gilkenson wrote, "With the air of an announcer 30 years his senior in experience, Johnnie meticulously and accurately goes about his duties under the guidance of his father..."[92]

---

[92] *Providence Sunday Journal*, October 15, 1961, p. 19.

Through the years, Gianpaolo continued to assist his father with the radio programs until he graduated college and moved to New York City, to work as an actor off Broadway. Returning to Rhode Island in 1995, Gianpaolo, while continuing to act at local and area theaters, would intermittently do some announcing on his father's radio program. Gianpaolo, however, was not the only Petrella child who inherited the entertainment gene. Rolando and Paola's youngest son, Dean, also answered the call to perform. Dean Petrella is currently the lead singer and guitarist of a local rock band known as "The Complaints." Their Facebook page describes the band as "a modern rock band led by guitarist/frontman Dean Petrella, with bassist Chris Cruz, and drummer Anthony Marotti. Their music is like audio comfort food — it's new, but familiar."[93] The title of one of the band's full-length albums, *Sunday Morning Radio*, is a reference to Petrella's father's radio program at WRIB which aired every Sunday morning from 10:30 a.m. to 1:00 p.m.

While producing his program *Piccolo Mondo* at WWRI, Rolando Petrella, would do a weekly reprise of the show at WKFD at 1370 kHz in Wickford, Rhode Island. Having spent two years at WKFD, in 1967 Rolando Petrella returned to his roots at WRIB, where he renamed his program *La Voce d'Italia* (*The Voice of Italy*). WRIB would become the home of *La Voce d'Italia* until the year 2000. Following Antonio Pace's sale of WRIB, Claudio Campellone and Rolando Petrella returned to the radio station to continue the Italian programming which was the foundation of the station. Campellone's *Festa Italiana* aired every Sunday from 10:30 a.m. to 11:30 a.m., followed by Petrella's *La Voce d'Italia*, from 11:30 a.m. until 1:30 p.m. Campellone remained with WRIB for two years, before

---

[93]   https://www.facebook.com/pg/The-Complaints-51669637600/about/?ref=page_internal.

moving his program to WHIM. Petrella, however, established WRIB as his home station and became increasingly involved in the management and administration of the station. Beginning in 1970, Petrella's *La Voce d'Italia* occupied the full four-hour spot from 10:30 a.m. to 1:30 p.m. He was listed as station manager from 1970 until 1975, and Italian programing increased from four hours to six hours.[94] Subsequently, Petrella's program, in addition to the Sunday schedule, aired Monday through Friday from 1:00 p.m. to sunset. This schedule endured into the early nineties when the program changed to a weekend format, airing on Saturday from 11:00 a.m. to 1:00 p.m., and Sunday 10:30 a.m. to 1:00 p.m.

Much like the American Grammy Awards, the *Festival di Sanremo* is an annual contest and award festival honoring the best popular musicians and songs in Italy. The festival began in January of 1951 and is held each year in the Italian Riviera city of Sanremo. To the delight of the Italian American community of Rhode Island, each February, Petrella would feature the annual *Festival di Sanremo* during his Sunday broadcasts, keeping his listeners informed about which singers and music groups were winning the festival and bringing the latest Italian hits to the community. For the spiritual enrichment of his listeners, Petrella also instituted a brief religious segment on Sunday mornings during which Padre Pietro Polo, a Scalabrini priest and pastor of the Holy Ghost Church in Providence, would read a gospel passage followed by a few brief comments on the reading. This short segment became a very popular feature of Petrella's Sunday broadcasts.

In the early eighties, a young, exciting voice joined Petrella at the microphone. Mariagina Aiello joined WRIB in 1982 as Petrella's co-host and quickly became very po-

---

[94] See *Broadcasting Yearbook 1970*, p. B-178; 1971, p. B-183; 1972, p. B185: 1973, p. B-177.

pular with listeners. While listeners still delighted in hearing the calm, velvet tones of Rolando's voice, Mariagina's voice was a fresh, new element which brought excitement to the program. The two co-hosted *La Voce d'Italia* until Petrella became very ill in 1997. During this time, Gianpaolo, now using the name John Paul, would also intermittently host the program. He and Aiello, however, never aired together.

Capitalizing on his popularity as a radio personality, Rolando Petrella ventured into other categories of entertainment in an effort to link his fellow Italo-Americans to their *patria*. One opportunity came through play producer Commendatore Rocco DeRusso, whose plays were performed in Italian. In a Play Bill dated Tuesday, April 1, 1958, DeRusso presented *The Passion Play*, and listed as "the impersonator of Christ" was signor Rolando Petrella. Petrella, however, did not limit himself to acting. In 1960, Petrella began what would become a busy endeavor of promoting popular Italian singers in Rhode Island theaters. On May 4, 1960, Petrella presented the famous Neapolitan singer Renato Carosone at the Uptown Theater in Providence. In 1962, the Uptown Theater was renamed the Columbus Theater, and program pamphlets from that era show Petrella offering performances by Italian singer/actress Milva on January 12, 1964; Italian superstar Claudio Villa on October 25, 1964; and singing sensation Sergio Bruni on November 14, 1964. Winning the *Festival di Sanremo* in 1955, Claudio Villa became one of Italy's most famous singers, recording over 3,000 songs and selling more than 45 million records during his career. He also performed in twenty-five musicals. Villa, at Petrella's behest, would return to Rhode Island twice in 1970, once in January at the Columbus Theater, and again in April, where he performed at the Veterans Memorial Auditorium. While in Providence, Villa stayed at the Petrella home, and as a special treat to his listeners, Rolando interviewed Villa live on *La Voce d'Italia*.

A gala celebration on February 11, 1967, marked the opening of the Italy Cinema at 910 Atwood Avenue in Johnston, Rhode Island. The theater, which began showing films prior to the Second World War, occupied the second floor of a strip of stores known as Ferri's Block. Rolando Petrella, in 1971, leased the theater and one of the store fronts directly beneath it. On the first floor, he established an Italian pastry shop and renamed the theater Cinema Italia. Each Sunday at 3:00 p.m. and 6:30 p.m., Cinema Italia offered the latest films from Italy as well as Italian classics. Local lore recounts that, once a month, "the boys" from Providence would visit Petrella's pastry shop to collect what was clandestinely known as protection money. They took more, however, than the "agreed upon" fee. Each month they would help themselves to a dozen or two of the pastries Petrella had for sale. As a former member of the Italian Special Police Force, Petrella well understood the unwritten rules of the underworld, and while he begrudgingly paid the fee, he never complained. The forfeiting of the pastry, however, was quite another matter. Having endured the theft of his pastry for several months, Petrella paid a visit to the office of crime boss Raymond Patriarca on Atwells Avenue in Providence who was an enthusiastic fan and patron of Petrella's radio program. Explaining to Patriarca that he had no problem with the monthly fee, he added that the loss of the pastry was deeply cutting into his profits and asked if the *don* could help. Petrella was promised that the problem would be resolved. The following month "the boys" arrived to make the collection. They neither asked for nor mentioned any pastry. Having collected the money, they left quietly. The issue ceased to exist. Cinema Italia continued to entertain the Italian American community until February of 1974, at which time the strip of stores was razed and the property sold. Undaunted, Petrella moved his cinema operation to the Hillside Cinema on Waterman Avenue in North Providence, offering Italian films during the same time slots as his defunct Cinema Italia.

One of the fondest memories Rhode Islanders have of Rolando Petrella is of the live readings of classic Italian authors which he would present throughout the state. Often, Petrella would be invited to read excerpts of Petrarca, Boccaccio, Macchiaveli, or several other famous Italian authors. He would present these readings at one of the meetings of the Order of the Sons of Italy, at the Aurora Civic Association, or at the Italo-American Club in Providence. While these presentations were always well received, his most popular readings were of Dante's *Commedia*. Whether it be for excerpts from the *Inferno*, *Purgatorio*, or *Paradiso*, people would gather in large groups for the chance to hear Rolando Petrella read select *canti* by Dante Alighieri.

Petrella was not only well-known for his radio program but also for the many charitable activities in which he engaged. In 1965, The St. Francis Cabrini (Italian) Church was established in Bedford, England, after a long fundraising campaign of which Rolando Petrella was one of the chief fundraisers. As a successful fundraiser, Petrella employed his abilities to raise funding for many orphanages in Italy and the United States, and through his radio program and many contacts, he provided disaster relief to many victims of Italian earthquakes. In addition to raising funds for Italian orphanages and disaster relief, Petrella was also an ardent supporter of many Italian organizations in Rhode Island. Religious and social societies such as The Papa Giovanni XXIII Society, the Scalabrini Villa Guild, The St. Mary's Feast Society, the Pontecorvo Society, The St. Anthony Society, and the Santa Maria di Prata Society, all claimed Petrella as a member. Philanthropically, he was no less active, as he served on the boards of United Italian

Americans (UNITAM), La Scuola d'italiano of Rhode Island, the Aurora Civic Association, the Italo American Club of Rhode Island, the Muscular Dystrophy Association, Meeting Street School, and the Impossible Dream Foundation. The President of Italy, Oscar Luigi Scalfaro, in 1992 awarded Petrella the Title of "Cavalliere," in order, as the *Providence Journal* wrote, to acknowledge all he did "to merit the Republic of Italy and for his outstanding service to the Italian community of Rhode Island."[95]

Rolando Petrella's radio career took a much different course early in 1997 when he was diagnosed with cancer. With the help of Mariagina Aiello and his son John Paul, Petrella continued to produce and host *La Voce d'Italia* as he underwent chemo and radiation therapy. Approximately five months before his death, in a very touching and poignant broadcast, John Paul and Rolando Petrella co-hosted Rolando's final show, which aired in July of 1998. Toward the end of the program, Rolando thanked his listeners for their many years of dedication, and the "serene well wishes" with which they had welcomed John Paul back to the program. Petrella stated, "Credo che sia normale sentire la vostra mancanza, dopo tanti anni che ci facciamo reciproca compagnia. Intanto vi ringrazio per il bene placido che avete nei riguardi di mio figlio."[96] John Paul, in expressing his heartfelt comments, added, "I believe it takes a lot of courage to first of all, stand up and fight this terrible malady, and second, and perhaps more importantly, it takes even more courage to face such a crisis with honesty and hope. Of course, I expect no less of him; he is, after all, my dad. So let me end by saying, Thanks, Dad.

---

[95] *Providence Journal*, Dec. 13, 1998.
[96] "I believe it is normal to feel this sense of loss, especially after so many years in which we've kept each other company. For now, I thank you for the serene well wishes which you have regarding my son."

Thanks for being an example for all of us to emulate. I believe if we can take our cue from you, we'll all be OK."[97]

Rolando Petrella died on December 9, 1998, thus ending an era in which the three pioneers, Antonio Pace, Claudio Campellone, and Petrella, delighted, informed, and entertained Rhode Island's Italo-Americans who came to depend on their broadcasts and their friendship. Their legacy remains an important element in the history of the Italian American community of Rhode Island and one which has endured into the twenty-first century.

---

[97] A recorded copy of this program exists in the Special Collections Area of the URI Library.

Chapter Six

TRANSITIONING FROM *LA VIA VECCHIA* TO THE NEW MILLENNIUM

MariaGina Aiello

> *"Noi italiani all'estero siamo una ricchezza per il nostro paese, l'Italia, e lo dimosteremo."*
>
> *MariaGina Aiello*

Johnny Nardo

> *"Nardolillo's passion for big-band music began when he was a teenager...when other kids were listening to disco or punk, he was collecting records by Harry James, Gene Krupa, Tommy Dorsey and, of course, Sinatra."*
>
> *Providence Journal*[98]

MARIAGINA AIELLO

In a front page article in the *Providence Journal*, entitled *TV Women:Extra Burdens*, journalist Donna Van Alst details some of the hurdles that female radio and television personalities had to endure as they became ever more present on the air. Van Alst, in her article, interviews former news anchor Sara Wye, who joined WJAR in Providence in 1973. Ann Conway of WLNE-TV Channel 6 is also quoted.[99] These women, along with Meredith Vieira, Patrice Wood, and Karen Adams, are among a list of successful journalists who paved the way for female radio and television announcers in the Ocean State. Enter

---

[98] See S.I. Rosenbaum, "'Yours truly, Johnny Nardo'" *Providence Journal*, June 18, 2002, p. C-01.

[99] *TV Women: Extra Burdens* by Donna Van Alst, *Providence Journal*, August 2, 1983, p. A-01.

MariaGina Aiello. A young immigrant from Palermiti in Calabria, Italy, MariaGina arrived in Providence with her parents in 1970. She studied journalism at the University of Rhode Island, and in 1982, Rolando Petrella invited Aiello to do some announcing for him on his radio program *La Voce d'Italia*. As a female, Aiello brought a new perspective to *La Voce d'Italia* in an age when female radio and television announcers were growing more popular. Aiello, a professional journalist, was the perfect compliment to Petrella,[100] and together they produced one of the most popular foreign language radio shows in Rhode Island.

As Petrella aged, Aiello took on increased responsibilities at WRIB, and after Petrella's death in 1998, MariaGina Aiello became the solo host of *The Voice of Italy* which remained at WRIB until the year 2000. Aiello, at that time, moved the program to WELH 88.1 FM in Providence, and began to collaborate with Radio Italia. In an effort to reach out to Italophiles who did not speak Italian but had a love and interest in Italy and its culture, Aiello changed the format to a bilingual program. Aiello renamed the show *The Voice of Italy's Radio Italia*, and in addition to the latest hits from Italy, she reported the news and current events. The program aired on Sundays from 12:00 p.m. until 2:00 p.m. During this time, Aiello often invited local high school students studying Italian to join her at the microphone to do some announcing in Italian. On several occasions, students from St Mary's Bay View Academy made fifteen-to-twenty-minute presentations much to the delight of their school community, their parents, and Aiello's listeners. In an interview with Dr. Ed Iannuccilli, Aiello explained that the mission of her radio show was to "keep you updated, entertained, and informed about the topics dear to me and

---

[100] There exists, in the Special Collections Area of the URI Library, a recorded copy of a program from January 26, 1992 with Petrella and Aiello at the mike.

those like me: Italy; its history, its culture, its people and therefore, our very identity. It is not an encyclopedic or literary undertaking; it is a transparent presentation of who I am (we are) and where I (we) come from."[101]

The Voice of Italy's Radio Italia remained with WELH until 2011, at which time the station was sold to the local NPR station, and the program was cancelled. Aiello's bilingual program had signaled a change for the Italian American community of Rhode Island. As the second, third, and fourth generations of Italian Americans assimilated, the Italian language radio program, broadcast entirely in the *madre lingua*, no longer attracted the faithful listeners as it had in the past. MariaGina Aiello, even with her innovative bilingual programing, and outreach to younger Italian Americans of the state, was having difficulty sustaining interest. She was not ready, however, to give up that easily. In 2012, she reestablished *The Voice of Italy* on station WPRV 790 AM, but this proved to be a very brief run.

Aside from her radio productions, Aiello served as executive assistant to the Italian Vice-Consulate of Rhode Island from 1999 to 2008. In 2011, she created the Italian Cultural Foundation of Rhode Island[102] in order to help promote the Italian culture throughout Rhode Island and New England. Beginning in April of 2017 until January of 2018, MariaGina was the host of *Bravissima*, a bilingual broadcast which aired every Sunday from 9:00 a.m. to 9:00 p.m., on RadioRI.net. Unfortunately, the website is presently defunct. MariaGina Aiello, however, remains undeterred in her effort to carry on the legacies of the Rhode Island Italian radio announcers who preceded her as she continues to search for a radio station interested in an Italian radio program.

---

[101] https://growingupitalian.wordpress.com/page/6/
[102] https://www.italiachiamaitalia.it/italiani-allestero-usa-maria-gina-aiello-coordina trice-dello-stato-del-rhode-island/.

JOHNNY NARDO

As a young man growing up in the Knightsville section of Cranston, RI, John Nardolillo Jr. had always dreamt of becoming a radio personality. After many years, and with a little help from his friend Chuck Stevens, Nardolillo's dream was fulfilled.

After graduating from Cranston High School West, Nardolillo attended Roger Williams University, where he majored in Criminal Justice. Upon graduation from university, he entered the Johnston Police Academy and served as an officer on the Johnston police force. Nardolillo was chosen by his colleagues to serve as president of the Johnston Police Union, an office he held for several years.

In May of 1983, John married Linda Hein.[103] John and Linda have two sons, Angelo and Vito. While Nardolillo enjoyed a successful career as a policeman, his desire to work in radio never abated. As a young college student, Nardolillo began to deejay at events and parties in the Cranston and Providence area. As Nardolillo honed his DJ skills, the popular Rhode Island radio personality Chuck Stevens, who was a close friend of John Nardolillo, Sr. -- affectionately known in Knightsville as Johnny Boots -- took John Jr. under his tutelage and began to teach him the radio business. Stevens,[104] one of the legends of Rhode Island radio, became famous in the 1950s at WRIB, spinning Rock and Roll records and opining on the new heartthrob named Elvis Presley. He later worked at WGNG AM 550, which in 1985 changed its call letters to WICE.[105] It was at WICE AM that Stevens began to tutor John Nardolillo, and it was at WICE 89.3 FM where

---

[103] See *The Providence Journal*, June 5, 1983, p. E-04.
[104] Charles Abajian, Jr., whose radio name was Chuck Stevens, was inducted into the Rhode Island Radio Hall of Fame in 2008. See the Rhode Island Radio Hall of Fame website at http://jrooke.tripod.com/rhodeislandradiohalloffame/id4.html.
[105] See *Broadcasting Yearbook 1986*, P. B-248.

Nardolillo's dream came to fruition. The "new" WICE FM was located in Johnston, RI, and owned by Steven Conti,[106] who also worked at WHJY 94.1 FM. In 1997, Nardolillo began to produce and broadcast his own radio show at the Johnston station. Hosted under his radio name Johnny Nardo, the show, entitled *Weekend Dance Party*, aired every Friday night for two hours. The show featured music from the Golden Age of the Big Band era showcasing Tommy Dorsey, Glen Miller, Duke Ellington, Matt Munroe, Frank Sinatra, and many others. The *Weekend Dance Party* remained with WICE FM until January of 1999 when the station went off air. Nardolillo moved his show to WELH 88.1 FM in Providence. He expanded the show to four hours, and it aired every Saturday from 3:00 p.m. until 7:00 p.m. The *Weekend Dance Party* became a very popular radio program bringing Johnny Nardo the satisfaction he had always sought while at the mic. The *Weekend Dance Party* remained at WELH until 2011 when the station became a repeater for the Rhode Island NPR station, which broadcasts from Union Station in Providence.

While in search of a host station, Johnny Nardo broadcasted for brief periods at several Rhode Island radio stations such as WRIU at the University of Rhode Island, WAKX, and WJZS. Finally, in early 2012, Nardo began broadcasting from WADK AM 1540 in Newport, RI. This new home afforded Nardo the opportunity to develop one of his ideas. Johnny Nardo believed that the Italian American community would appreciate a new type of Italo-American radio show, one which would underscore its pride in its Italian heritage, while simultaneously remaining distinct-

---

[106] See Celeste Katz's article "FCC Sinks Pirate Station WICE, which Entertained Johnston Listeners for 3 ½ Years, Is Off the Air," *The Providence Journal*, January 20, 1999, p. C-01. Also, Thomas J. Morgan's article "Mystery Radio Station Baffles FCC, and Listeners," *Providence Journal*, February 19, 1997, p. C-04.

ly American. He began to produce and host a very specialized program the format of which catered to second and third generation Italian Americans. This program is entitled *That's Amore*, taking its name from the song made famous by Dean Martin. The program is broadcast in English with a sprinkling of Italian phrases which serve to underscore the Italo-American theme of the show. While Nardo presents music from Italy, it is mostly nostalgic music such as songs sung by Claudio Villa, Domenico Modugno, Luciano Pavarotti, and Andrea Bocelli. The majority of the artists Nardo features on his program, however, are Italian American singers from the fifties and sixties. Listeners are treated to crooners such as Frank Sinatra, Dean Martin, Jerry Vale, as well as entertainers Lou Monte, and Louis Prima. Interspersed among the music, Nardo entertains his listeners with Italian American comedians such as Pat Cooper. Nardo, well known for his interview capabilities, often interviews famous entertainers on his program. Some of the more popular have been his interviews with Connie Francis, Julius LaRosa, Jimmy Roselli, Al Martino, and Jerry Vale.

That's Amore spent one year in Newport at WADK and then moved to Westerly, RI, to WBLQ AM 1230. The program airs every Sunday morning from 9:00 a.m. to 11:00 a.m. and has become extremely popular throughout the Rhode Island Italo-American community, as it seems to be the follow up to MariaGina Aiello's bilingual program. Its target is an English-speaking audience, who harbors great pride in its Italian American roots, but unfortunately, is very limited in the *madre lingua*. Nardo begins each broadcast with a brief comedy clip from one of Pat Cooper's albums immediately followed by the introduction theme song *The Whole World Loves Italians* sung by Sam Buttera. As Nardo signs off each week, Andrea Bocelli is heard in the background singing his famous *Con Te Partirò*. Throughout the broadcast, Nardo continues to conjure up nostalgic memories for his listeners. One of his more famous lines is, "We're going back in time, to the good olds of Sunday mornings and mamma's kitchen." He often encourages his listeners to contact him with the following invitation: "Hey, drop me an email and tell me what you put in your gravy." (Gravy is what most Italo-Americans in RI call tomato sauce.) In an interview for the *Providence Journal*, Nardo once explained that he is very fond of remembering his youth and the culture in which he was raised. "'I like the nostalgia,' he said. 'I'm the kind of guy who likes to go back in time... I feel like I missed something. I feel like I've been there.'"[107]

After retiring from the Johnston Police Force, Nardolillo served as a police officer for the town of West Greenwich, RI. In 2000, Nardolillo was elected to the Cranston City Council, and served as the chairman of the council's Finance Committee. Nardolillo also served as president of the St. Mary's Feast Society, which is responsible for organizing an annual festival in honor of the Virgin Mary. Having been involved in many diverse occupations and activities, Nardolillo claims that he is happiest at the microphone entertaining his loyal radio audience. While his radio program may not be broadcast in the Italian language, Johnny Nardo continues to bear the torch lit so many years ago by the pioneers of Italian radio in Rhode Island.

---

[107] S.I. Rosenbaum, "Yours truly, Johnny Nardo," *Providence Journal*, June 18, 2020, p. C-01.

EPILOGUE

Having discussed the pioneers of the Rhode Island Italo-American community in both print and radio, it is important to mention some of the lesser-known announcers as well, those whose programs aired on smaller stations, and did not enjoy the many years of programming as did the aforementioned announcers. One of the foremost of these announcers is Nino Di Salle, who hosted an Italian music program on WXTR AM 550 (originally WPAW).[108] Di Salle was a deputy sheriff for Providence County, who, in his youth, acted on the vaudeville stage. Di Salle was the director of the Fine Arts Opera Theater and had served as executive manager of the Veterans Memorial Auditorium in Providence, Rhode Island. Nino Di Salle's program, *The Italian Morning Parade*, first aired in 1955 on Sunday mornings from 8:00 to 9:00 on WPAW AM 550, then moved to the 9:30 to 11:00 slot beginning in 1958. *The Italian Morning Parade* ran until Di Salle's death in March of 1964.

Professor Salvatore Scotti and his wife Linda hosted a radio program entitled *Roman Holiday*. Graduating from the University of Rome with a doctorate in chemistry, Dr. Scotti immigrated to America in 1947. He came to Rhode Island where his father, Dr. Luigi Scotti, was a practicing physician. Dr. Salvatore Scotti was hired by Providence College to teach Italian, a position he held for 27 years. Linda and Salvatore founded the Scot-Tussin Pharmacal Co. in 1954 after one of their daughters suffered from a persistent cough.[109] The Scottis brought their daughter to a specialist who prescribed a suppressant which alleviated

---

[108] *The Providence Journal*, March 21, 1964, p. 18.
[109] Arthur S. Reseigh, "Pharmaceutical Line Began With One Item," *The Providence Sunday Journal, Rhode Island's Magazine of Business Finance Industry*, September 20, 1964, pp. 1, 26-27.

the child's cough. This situation led Dr. Scotti to begin research on his own version of a cough syrup and eventually the founding of the Scot-Tussin Pharmacal Company. In the midst of raising a family, creating pharmaceutical products, and teaching Italian, Salvatore and Linda found time to produce a weekly radio program, *Roman Holiday*, which aired on WYNG AM 1590 on Sunday mornings from 9:00 a.m. to 10:00 a.m. In 1968, the radio station changed its call letters to WARV, and *Roman Holiday* continued to air until 1970.

The Music of Italy aired every Sunday from 3:00 p.m. to 4:00 p.m. on WARV in Warwick, Rhode Island. The show was produced and hosted by Nicholas DiPietro, who emigrated from Pollutri, in the Abruzzo region of Italy. DiPietro settled in Cranston, Rhode Island.[110] He served as account executive of the *Italian Echo* newspaper, and later held the same position at the *Cranston Mirror* newspaper. In 1960, DiPietro began to produce a radio program entitled *The Italo-American Hour*, which was broadcast on WYNG AM 1590 from 8:00 a.m. to 9:00 a.m. In 1968, when the station changed to WARV, DiPietro's show moved to the 3:00 p.m. time slot, and he renamed the show *The Music of Italy*.

On March 19, 1995, in celebration of St. Joseph's Day, a group of friends took to the airwaves on WNRI 1380 AM in Woonsocket, Rhode Island. To celebrate the feast day the group, in a live radio broadcast, played instruments and sang Italian songs. The show was an immediate success with area listeners and was subsequently scheduled to air on the fourth Tuesday of every month from 6:00 p.m. to 7:30 p.m.[111] Charles Baldelli, former mayor of Woonsocket, hosted the program which he called *Buon Giorno* and

[110] *The Providence Journal*, August 10, 1982, p. C-02.
[111] Patricia Russell, "Live, on the air, Italian Radio Impromptu Radio Show Proves Listener-friendly," *The Providence Journal*, December 10, 1998.

would open each show by greeting his listeners with, "Buongiorno a tutti quanti, io sono il sindaco Charlie Baldelli."[112] The group, also known as "The Crew," consisted of six friends: Mayor Baldelli, Tony Vetri (on the harmonica), Ed "Chico" Ciccone (on the keyboard), Kenneth Bianchi, Velmo "Mo" Chiaverini, and Charles Desaulniers, whom Baldelli called "Carlo the Crooner." Later, Vincenzo Fiontella replaced Ed Ciccone at the keyboard, and Connie "Concetta" Gautheir joined The Crew. Unrehearsed and unscripted, *Buon Giorno* had a party-like atmosphere with Mo Chiaverini serving as resident comedian. Baldelli remembers fondly, "We just did it to have a good time. Mo would keep everyone laughing and the audience loved it."[113] Interspersed among the Crew's live "performance," Baldelli would play recordings by classic Italian singers such as Carlo Buti and Claudio Villa.

The Crew often brought their show on the road playing at area Italian social clubs like the Italian Workmen's Club in Woonsocket, RI, as well as clubs in Milford, Massachusetts. *Buon Giorno* aired on WNRI for five years, into the beginning of the new century. Baldelli says that people still stop him today to reminisce about all the fun they had listening to *Buon Giorno* every month.[114]

The language of any given culture is the foundation of that culture, and it is through their language that the people find their true identity. The French anthropologist Claude Levi-Strauss argued that language is the means through which culture is transmitted. It becomes extremely difficult, and perhaps impossible, to preserve a culture if the language is lost. When people say, "I'm Italian, but I don't speak Italian," they create a disconnect between themselves and the *patria*. Is the Italo-American community of Rhode

---

[112] "Good day everyone, I am the mayor, Charlie Baldelli."
[113] From a telephone interview with former mayor of Woonsocket Charles Baldelli. May 20, 2020.
[114] Ibid.

Island able to retain its culture and pass it on to the next generation of Italian Americans when a majority of its people lack even a basic knowledge of the *madre lingua*? While radio hosts of the past like Antonio Pace, Claudio Campellone, and Rolando Petrella produced programs which served as news, information, and entertainment for the Italian immigrants, today's Italo-Americans need Italian language newspapers and radio programs to pre-serve the beautiful language and culture of our ancestors and to educate future generations of Italian Americans in Rhode Island.

PHOTOS

Antonio Pace in his radio studio at WRIB

Antonio Pace, in Italy, recording a women's greeting to her family in Rhode Island

Claudio Campellone

Claudio Campellone in the studio at WKRI

Italia ⊕ U.S.A.

VOL. 2, No.15. ©1994 ITALIA ⊕ U.S.A. PUBLISHING INC. • Telephone # 946-1981 • FAX# 944-8570 November 4, 1994

What's Inside

Rhode Island's Italian Americans
The Heritage

By Joe Fuoco

Every Italian house knows a wooden rolling pin. And there is one at the Roger Williams Park Museum.

Local Ties, RI's Italian American is an exhibit that is an opening for the large exhibition of Italian- American Folklife in the West, profiled in our last issue.

The Roger Williams Park Museum has put together a moving, evocative, and very nostalgic exhibit that should be embraced by all Italian Americans in the state, for the exhibit is about them, their ancestors, the people who came from the villages, largely from the south of Italy to make a new life.

Here one sees the magnificent wedding portrait of

Caprini family, turn of the century
Photo courtesy of Joseph and Mary Caprini

A townload of memories and dreams

Giovanna Corvese and Enricillo Caduss, a photograph of Joe Caprara's ancestors with a family tree showing relationships: Joe and his wife Marge have loaned to this exhibit treasures, magnificently preserved mementos of their parents who were the immigrants in that great wave that came to America. There are the Italian passports of Marge's parents, a beautiful trando photograph of children, the passport of Elvira Cicchelli

who married Vincenzo DiRaimo, who died four sons and a daughter, and who sees a connection, a part of so many.

When one sees and recognizes a name, when you know the people, there is a special intimacy, a special warmth. Elvira and Vincenzo were my neighbors. They were there on the top of the hill of a street called Tiffany in Cranston, in the Thornton section. Elvira was the soul of the family, its heart. They worked hard, very hard as these people are born to work, they planted gardens, the fireplaces in the living room of the book house was a mosaic of polished stones. Elvira was the one who listened, who gave advice.

... who knew, and to the museum, to see their passports, the old pictures is to possess a part of their lives.

continued on page 5

Grazzanise Celebrates Little Alessandro
Out of Horror The Gift of Life

By Raffaele Raimondo

Ed. Note : The following is an article translated from Italian, written by an Italian journalist Raffaele Raimondo. The story is a very current one, dealing with Alessandro Vitolo, an eight year old Italian boy whose life was saved by a bone marrow transplant donated by Marlene and Bruce McGarvey of New Jersey. The marrow came from their son, brutally killed in a crossfire in Sicily. The McGarveys donated various organs from their son to help other human beings. Thus, out of the unthinkable tragedy of their son's death has come life for others.

Grazzanise, a town in the province of Caserta, has recently held a great celebration for a little boy who underwent a successful bone marrow transplant, fighting against all odds.

His house, already of recent construction was completely repainted and everything was in order to celebrate the new life of Alessandro, a child of Grazzanise, a child whose wanderings throughout Italy and abroad have been kept out of the press for two years.

Maybe because we kept our fingers crossed, maybe not to intrude into the sufferings and sacrifices of the parents Nicola and Antonietta Vitolo, but also to respect the wishes of the grandparents, uncles, brothers and cousins among whom is Teresa, who easily comes to tears when she talks about Alessandro.

But the stoic participation to the exceptional event came from the whole community of Grazzanise. Let's be honest. A bone marrow transplant in the United States of America inspires the mobilization of energies and organizations of the outmost spectrum.

Just think of the river of money that was necessary and the huge generosity required to accomplish such a task.

The success of the transplant brought joy to the institutions and the thousands of people who have been involved.

Since the beginning, when Alessandro was two years old, Dr. Rosa D'Amore, of the Polyclinic in Naples and Prof. Auriechio, director of the polyclinic, continue to follow

Alessandro.

Dr. Sebastiano Trombacco, who practices surgery in the city of Warwick, Rhode Island, two years ago did the impossible ("I salti mortali"), when he collaborated in the search for a donor to donate bone marrow for Alessandro.

For a period (of time) this case has been followed in America also by a doctor Eduardo Lanino from Centro Trapianti del Gaslini in Genova who, at the time, was in the United States for research and studies.

The list of experts in the field of medicine would be too long to describe, so many have been the procedures performed in this ordeal blessed by God.

continued on page 5

Italia/USA newspaper, November 4, 1994

93

L'ECO DEL RHODE ISLAND.

GIORNALE SETTIMANALE CHE VIEN DATO GRATIS.

ANNO I. N° 1.   PROVIDENCE, R. I., SABATO 2 OTT°°BRE, 1897.   IL TIPOGRAFO, F. CURZIO.

SALUTATORY.

After a careful study of the Italian Colony of Providence, its customs and traits, together with the interest that it takes and ought to take in public affairs, I have come to the conclusion that an Italian newspaper "published with the sole intention of furthering the interest of the Colony cannot be anything but a success. It is not a new conception, it has been tried before, and has failed: but the ideas of the gentleman who undertakes to publish L'ECO DEL RHODE ISLAND, differs entirely from those of the gentlemen who were interested in previous enterprises of this sort.

The present newspaper will be called L'ECO DEL RHODE ISLAND. The main interest of the founders of this paper will be:

1st—To pacify and mediate all the heated controversies now existing in the Colony.

2nd—To instruct those that lack knowledge of the English language, in the current affairs of City and State.

3rd—To guard the colony from infamous and false attacks heretofore launched by certain brainless and know-nothing men.

4th—To make public all the interesting happenings of the day.

The Paper will issued every Saturday; it will be distributed FREE among the Italians of Providence, only postage will be charged to Italians residing in the State of Rhode Island, outside of the City of Providence, making it therefore one of the best mediums of advertising for those who wish to reach the Italians for the furthering of business.

It will be published in Italian, except a column or so; which will be in English, and in it, an account of Italy and Italian's customs, laws, and habits will be fully described.

It will never touch subjects pertaining to religion.

Politically it will stand on the side of the party that made the United States a great nation, and which is even now striving to make the star spangled banner respected and revered the whole world over.

It will combat all the perverse sectarianism with incessant energy. It will praise the worthy, blame the worthless. Any question asked will be answered according to the history, statistics, or common sense, provided it is of a nature that no harm will come to decency or personal character.

It will be the organ of the colony, its columns will be opened to every one, but it will invariably be closed for personal correspondence, or personal sentiments.

L'ECO DEL RHODE ISLAND will be published with the sole intention to do good, and if harm be done it will be because we do not know how to avert it; and with this opinion fixed on our minds we say forth ready to be favorably or adversely criticized.

A. R. S.

F. CURZIO, Editor.

Apprendiamo con vivo piacere, che l'Egregio amico nostro, Sig. F. S. Savarese, riassumerà la direzione del "Pro Patria" di New Haven col prossimo numero. Egli, che altra volta diresse la "Stella" e "Pro Patria" die' prouva della sua valentia come scrittore e giornalista provetto; fucciamo a lui giungere le nostre congratulazioni, le più sentite, e gli auguri di prosperità; dividio alla sua gentile Signora Yone Spold, pel contratto matrimonio, facendo voti che, tale avvenimento, sia apportatore di felicità e fortuna, che di cuore auguriano gli amici suoi.

Leggete il prossimo numero

Dell'Eco del R. I"

Sponsali e Battesimo.

Domenica scorsa, nella Chiesa Italiana, dal Rev. Padre Novati, fu celebrato il Matrimonio della Signorina Luisa Zambarano col Sig. Pietro Massa.

È superfluo dire che amici parenti e conoscenti, in gran numero si recarono a felicitare gli sposi —una bella coppia; che essi gli sposi ebbero dei belli e ricchi doni—la numerosa famiglia Zambarano, faceva gli onori di casa, senza trascurare mai nessuno.

Il Sig. Paolo Zambarano, padre della sposa, coadiuvato dalla sua gentile Signora, in mezzo alla brillante folla, si moltiplicavano nel badare a tutto e a tutti.

Fra le persone intervenute a quella festa di famiglia, notammo: Giuseppe Zambarano e Signora, Luigi-Zambarano e famiglia, Giovanni Zambarano [di New York, venuto per l'occasione]; Lorenzo Zambarano, Vincinzo Storti e famiglia, Frank Storti e famiglia, Giuseppe Storti e famiglia, Emilio D'Andre e famiglia, E. Gioatti e famiglia, F. Martelucci e Signora, Alfonso Ricci e famiglia, A. Sant'Antonio, D. Mariano e morella, ed altri che non ricordo i nomi.

Molte carrozze accompagnarono gli sposi alla Chiesa. La sera non mancò 'la Musica, con gli usuali quattro salti.

In quell'occasione, e nella stessa abituizone, si battezzò anche una bella e vezzosa bambina, ed il padrino fu il Sig. Frank Storti, e la madrina la Signora Maddalena Storti, moglie del Frank.

L'Eco del R. I. augura agli sposi una continua lusa di miele, senza interrussione, ed alla bambina che cresca secondo la volontà del padre, Sig. Paolo Zambarano, e della madre Signora Francesca Zambarano.

⁂

Giacche' siamo a Spruce St., ove abita la maggioranza della nostra Colonia, si avrà sempre piacere di vederci in festa:

Lunedì sera, 27 Settembre, [secondo il Lunario di Campitelli] ricorreva la festa di San Cosmo, e facevasi festa: la numerosa famiglia Bucci che si chiama Cosmo, non mancò, come sempre a far complimenti, a tutti gli amici che si recarono a visitarlo, nel suo Barr-Room; diversi musicanti, amici del San Cosmo, rallegrarono la conversazione, sonando scelti pezzi di buoni autori.

L'Eco, augura al Sig. Cosmo Bucci salute e dollari.

F. C.

Front page of the first issue of *L'Eco Del Rhode Island*, October 2, 1897

Front page of *The Italian Echo*, January 3, 1930

Inaugural issue of *The Rhode Island Italo-American,*
October 12, 1938

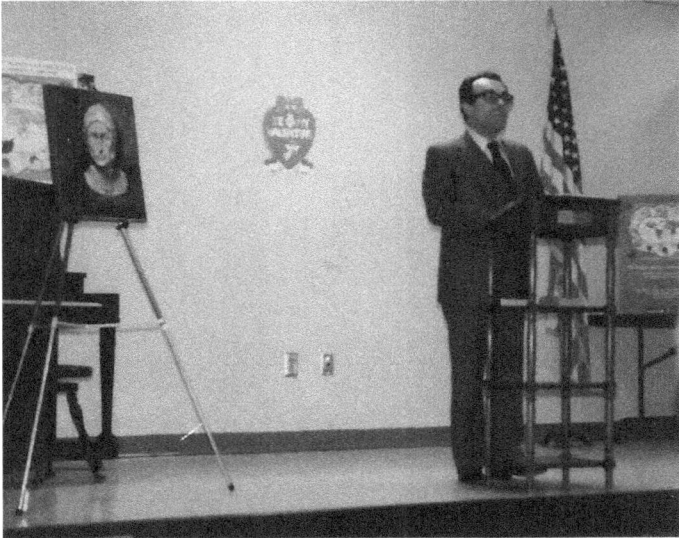

Rolando Petrella reading form Dante Alighieri's *Divine Comedy*

About the Author

ALFRED R. CRUDALE is a native Rhode Islander who grew up in the Knightsville section of Cranston. He has been an educator in Rhode Island for thirty-six years and earned his Ph.D. in Italian literature from the University of Connecticut. He and his wife Barbara, the parents of four boys, live on their small farm in West Kingston, Rhode Island.

ROBERT VISCUSI ESSAYS SERIES

Named in honor of the work of Robert Viscusi, this referred series is dedicated to the long essay. It intends to publish studies that are longer than the traditional journal-length essay and yet shorter than the traditional book-length manuscript. All books are peer-reviewed.

Linda L. Carroll. *Thomas Jefferson's Italian and Italian-Related Books in the History of Universal Personal Rights. An Overview.* Volume 1.

Luisa Del Giudice, ed. *Triangulations within the Italy-Canada-United States.* Volume 2.

ROBERT VISCUSI
—1941-2020—

Robert Viscusi was fundamental to the development of Bordighera Press; to its journal *VIA: Voices in Italian Americana*, and to the book series *VIA* FOLIOS.

One of his many ground-breaking articles, "Breaking the Silence: Strategic Imperatives for Italian American Culture," opened the *VIA*'s inaugural issue. In like fashion, his keenly satiric, genial long poem, "An Oration upon the Most Recent Death of Christopher Columbus," was the stimulus for the founding our first book series, *VIA* FOLIOS.

In later years we also published his epic poem, *Ellis Island*, a collection of sonnets whose "Star Review" from *Publishers Weekly*, that closed as follows: "[T]he sonnets are far from uniform, at times manifesting as short stories, at other times as short bursts of philosophical inquiry or bursts of pure song. This is a new delicacy for aficionados of creative poetry and an anthem of sorts for those who—however far removed from immigration—occasionally feel displaced from home."

www.ingramcontent.com/pod-product-compliance
Lightning Source LLC
Chambersburg PA
CBHW051733040426
42447CB00008B/1115